SYRIAN REFUGEE CHILDREN IN AUSTRALIA AND SWEDEN

Both Australia and Sweden are economically, socially and politically well-developed countries and each has responded to the Syrian crisis in its own way with features that define refugee children's schooling trajectories for transition to life and work. *Syrian Refugee Children in Australia and Sweden* provides insights into policies influencing the education and schooling of Syrian refugee children in Australia and Sweden.

This book uses the perspectives of Syrian refugee children and their voiced experiences to elicit recommendations for education practices and content. Their voices were central to the analysis for the main reason that their viewpoints could contribute in a practical way to the development of pedagogical approaches that would support their schooling, and an effective and productive transition to life in the host countries. The opinions, suggestions and experiences of other stakeholders, such as parents, caregivers, teachers and school and state officials, were included for greater understanding so that as many relevant contexts are covered.

The recommendations for refugee education proposed in this book will be useful for teachers, principals and policy makers directly involved in educating refugee students and this could positively impact on young refugee students finding their way to a new and better life.

Nina Maadad is a senior lecturer at the University of Adelaide. Her research interests include identity and marginalization of new arrivals, refugees particularly from non-Arabic-speaking backgrounds across the curricula, culture and education and languages.

SYRIAN REFUGEE CHILDREN IN AUSTRALIA AND SWEDEN

Education and Survival among the Displaced, Dispossessed and Disrupted

Nina Maadad

LONDON AND NEW YORK

First published 2020
by Routledge
2 Park Square, Milton Park, Abingdon, Oxon OX14 4RN

and by Routledge
52 Vanderbilt Avenue, New York, NY 10017

Routledge is an imprint of the Taylor & Francis Group, an informa business

© 2020 Nina Maadad

The right of Nina Maadad to be identified as author of this work has been asserted by him/her/them in accordance with sections 77 and 78 of the Copyright, Designs and Patents Act 1988.

All rights reserved. No part of this book may be reprinted or reproduced or utilised in any form or by any electronic, mechanical, or other means, now known or hereafter invented, including photocopying and recording, or in any information storage or retrieval system, without permission in writing from the publishers.

Trademark notice: Product or corporate names may be trademarks or registered trademarks, and are used only for identification and explanation without intent to infringe.

British Library Cataloguing in Publication Data
A catalogue record for this book is available from the British Library

Library of Congress Cataloging-in-Publication Data
A catalog record has been requested for this book

ISBN: 978-0-367-31303-6 (hbk)
ISBN: 978-0-367-31304-3 (pbk)
ISBN: 978-0-429-31619-7 (ebk)

Typeset in Bembo
by Taylor & Francis Books

 Printed in the United Kingdom by Henry Ling Limited

I dedicate this book to all the children who have been challenged and displaced and/or are still being challenged and displaced. I can only hope that life opens up brighter and safer futures ahead for them, so that they can enjoy a childhood that every child deserves, and provide them with equal opportunities to those that other children receive.

I would also like to remind all those in power or authority that their decisions – be it for resettlement, policies, strategies, humanitarian aid, education, etc. – can change the lives of the many millions of displaced people who are awaiting solutions for their situations.

May some of the suggestions shared in this book provide the guidance and assistance to support the refugee and asylum-seeker children, and most importantly, help make education equally profitable, available and accessible to everyone.

CONTENTS

List of figures   *x*
Acknowledgements   *xi*
Acronyms and abbreviations   *xii*
Preface   *xiii*

1   Introduction: Refugee children and education   1

    Preamble 1
    Syrian refugee children 3
    The right to education 6
    Why Australia and Sweden? 7
    Organisation of this book 9

2   Making education available to refugee children: Innovative theories and effective practices   14

    Introduction 14
    The challenge to make schooling available 15
    'As never before': The need for the education and schooling of refugee children 19
    Paulo Freire's Pedagogy of the Oppressed *as a theory for educating refugee children 20*
    Responding to refugee students' immediate needs 21
    Responding to refugee students' future-oriented needs 23

Countering moral panic-inspired Islamophobia 30
Conclusion 32

3   Methodology   37

   Introduction 37
   Case study design 38
   Data-collection methods 39
   Data analysis 42
   Conclusion 42

4   Policies and education for refugees in Australia   45

   Introduction 45
   Refugees and asylum seekers in Australia: a summary 47
   The post-war programme 48
   Education of refugee children 49
   The Australian Refugee and Humanitarian Program 51
   Australian education and refugee children 54
   Syrian refugee children in Australian schools – a snapshot 58
   Possible future challenges and recommendations 60

5   Policies and education for refugees in Sweden   70

   Introduction 70
   Statistical context 72
   Overview of education in Sweden for refugee children 74
   Syrian refugee children in Sweden's education and employment systems 76
   Possible future challenges and recommendations 78
   Conclusion 81

6   Discussion and comparison of refugee children in education in Australia and Sweden   86

   Classroom description 87
   Student–teacher relationship 87
   Second-language learning 89
   Personal stories and current situations 94
   Counsellors and psychologists 97
   Feelings about their host country 99
   Refugee children's thoughts about the future 102

7 Conclusion and recommendations 107

  Introduction 107
  General findings for Australia and Sweden 108
  Recommendations 113
  Final remarks 114

Appendix 119
Index 121

FIGURES

3.1 The critical paradigm concepts in the analysis of the two sets of data   43
A1 Pedagogy of the displaced   119
A2 Pedagogy of the displaced   120

ACKNOWLEDGEMENTS

First, I wish to express my sincere thanks and gratitude to my mentor and guide Dr Margaret Secombe. I am extremely grateful and indebted to her for her expert, sincere and valuable guidance and encouragement not only on this juncture but also all the way through my academic journey.

Second, I would like to place on record my sincere gratitude to Dr Grant Rodwell who was supposed to co-author this book with me, however, due to unfortunate family reasons he was not able to contribute on this occasion.

Third, I also sincerely thank all the participants, teachers, counsellors, principals, officials and staff members from Australia, Sweden and Lebanon for their contribution, guidance and time during my research.

I take this opportunity to thank my editor Mr Philip Thomas who went out of his way to help when required. I know that at times, I have 'interrupted his work patterns' but nonetheless, he was supportive and for that, I am grateful.

A big thank you also to my colleague and friend Dr Marizon Yu 'Queen of graphs' for her support.

Special appreciation and gratefulness goes to my husband Paul for putting up with my endless working hours and my son Ted for my withdrawal while working and I must admit that I do not know what I would do without you both and without your unconditional love and support.

Also a huge thank you to my mother, sisters, brother and uncle for giving me encouragement, enthusiasm and endless love.

I wish to formally acknowledge that some of the data and information about Australia used in Chapter 4 is the preliminary findings from a collaborative current study with the Centre for Lebanese Studies and the project donor is 'The Spencer Foundation'.

Finally, yet importantly, I wish to thank the University of Adelaide for providing me the time to embark on this opportunity.

ACRONYMS AND ABBREVIATIONS

ACTA	Australian Council of TESOL Associations
EALD	English as an additional language or dialect
ESL	English as a second language
EU	Council of the European Union
NGO	Non-governmental organisation
SAC	Special Assistance Category
UN	United Nations
UNHCR	United Nations High Commissioner for Refugees
UNICEF	United Nations International Children's Emergency Fund

PREFACE

In the second decade of the twenty-first century, more than half of any refugee population are children. First and foremost, refugee children are children and for this reason they require special attention. Increasingly, as the title of this book states, it is very evident that events in the Middle East are turning children into 'children of war', suffering from wars waged by adults. Only very recently, it was reported that: 'In Yemen, fighting continued to engulf the country, where up to 85,000 children have died of starvation' (Ronalds, 2019, p. 20). As refugees, they are especially at risk with the uncertainty and unprecedented upheavals that now characterise the post-Cold War era. The problems and challenges described in this book are not new, given that over two decades ago, in October 1993, the United Nations High Commissioner for Refugees adopted a Policy on Refugee Children, simply to improve refugee children's protection and care.

As this book describes in the pages that follow, there are more than 68.5 million refugees worldwide and more than 11 million are children; it was reported that in 2017 alone, the global number of people forcibly displaced from their homes was in effect 44,400 people every day (UNHCR, 2019). In writing this book, I was hit hard and repeatedly by the message that children are very vulnerable and susceptible to disease, malnutrition, physical injury and forms of abuse that range from the psychological to physical and sexual. Children are dependent creatures who desperately need the support of adults, not only for physical survival, particularly in the early years of childhood when education is so important, but also for their psychological and social well-being. Children grow in developmental sequences, much like a tree or plant with each growth spurt depending on the one before it. Serious delays interrupting these sequences can severely disrupt development.

Refugee children encounter far greater dangers to their safety and well-being – even the very real risk of death – than most children living in a wealthy Western country where they are generally well provided for. The sudden and violent onset of emergencies, the disruption of families and community structures, as well as the acute shortage of resources with which most refugees are confronted, deeply impact on the physical and psychological well-being of refugee children. Refugee children are among the most vulnerable in the world. Every day, they risk loss of some kind, including the loss of the future and hope that every child deserves. While homes and possessions can be replaced, children are irreplaceable. Many refugee children have been injured escaping their homeland. Others have been orphaned or have lost brothers and sisters, in ways that have robbed them of a happy childhood. It is important to remember not only that 4 million refugee children worldwide are currently out of school, but they are also subsequently vulnerable to discrimination and potential abuse, as well as exploitation by traffickers, or the pressure of having to enter into early marriage. In the aftermath of emergencies and in the search for solutions, the separation from families and familiar structures continues to affect adversely refugee children of all ages. Thus, helping refugee children to meet their physical and social needs often means providing support to their families and communities.

Much was reported in the media about the 2015/16 peak of refugee arrivals in Europe, before attention shifted to the issue of how to effectively integrate migrants into their new societies. This study also deals with the overarching theme of migration policy and – while it remains a national responsibility – it is evident that central and local authorities recognise that integration needs to happen where people are, in their workplaces, in their communities and neighbourhoods, and in the schools where they send their children. For all the statistics that are cited in this research, there are in fact individuals or families starting a new life in a new place. Local authorities, while coordinating with all levels of government and other local partners, play a major role in integrating newcomers and trying to give them the means and opportunities to contribute to their new communities.

While the media and public debates, most notably those occurring in Australia and Sweden, which are documented and compared in this book, have focused on the initial reception of migrants, recent increases in refugee arrivals have exposed the underlying governance weaknesses in both the short- and long-term responses for integration. Such weaknesses often stem from the lack of coordination among policies across different sectors (for instance labour, health, housing and education), as well as across levels of government. Recent events have also been a catalyst for public-sector, and especially education, innovation, so that refugee children are given a better chance, by bringing together and interviewing decision makers, teachers, parents and students. It is hoped that readers will engage with the inspiring examples to be found in this book.

References

Ronalds, Paul (2019). 'Say goodbye to the year of hell for children', *Advertiser*, 3 January, p. 20.
UNHCR (2019). *Global Trends: Forced Displacement in 2017*. Retrieved 25 February 2019 from www.unhcr.org/globaltrends2017/.

1
INTRODUCTION
Refugee children and education

Preamble

Throughout the world, more and more people are now on the move, fleeing war zones, escaping injustice and persecution or seeking better chances in life for themselves and their children. With the increase in global migration flows, the number of immigrants since the 1960s has more than tripled in Organisation for Economic Co-operation and Development countries. The increase in asylum-seeker movements to developed countries has resulted in an important and indeed seismic event during recent decades. These shifting migration processes have reshaped societies and politics, and have led to significant demographic changes in student populations. The major consequence is that educators face urgent needs in their classrooms; in particular, ensuring that all children have access to quality education has become a concern for education systems around the world.

In the twenty-first century, the provision of education opportunities for refugees is one of the highest priorities that all developed societies have a responsibility to deliver; millions of people have been forced to leave their home country due to war, economic failure, ethnic/racial rivalries, and changing environmental conditions. Briefly, the 1951 Convention Relating to the Status of Refugees states that:

> A refugee is someone who, owing to a well-founded fear of being persecuted for reasons of race, religion, nationality, membership of a particular social group, or political opinion, is outside the country of his (her) nationality, and is unable to or, owing to such fear, is unwilling to avail herself (himself) of the protection of that country.
>
> *(Educate a Child, n.d.)*

Furthermore the 1951 Refugee Convention and the 1967 Protocol (Relating to the Status of Refugees) set standards that are applicable to children in the same way as to adults: (1) a child who has a 'well-founded fear of being persecuted' for one of the stated reasons is a 'refugee'; (2) a child holding refugee status cannot be forced to return to the country of origin (the principle of non-refoulement); and (3) there is no distinction between children and adults regarding social welfare and legal rights. Article 22 of the convention sets standards which are of special importance to children: refugees must receive the 'same treatment' as nationals in primary education, and treatment at least as favourable as that provided to non-refugee aliens in secondary education (UNHCR, 1994, pp. 4–5; see also UNICEF, n.d.). However, according to Loprinzi (2016, p. 18), most 'contracting states' have not held up their part of the convention to assist the incoming refugee children's education. Instead, international organisations have to make up for the deficiencies of overwhelmed and under-resourced states like those in the European Union.

It is now the case that although Europe may not have expected the entry of a mass of refugees, such as those that have arrived in the last few years, they are now still responsible for them. The reality is that although some protracted refugee situations have lasted for more than two decades, the education of refugees is generally financed from emergency funds, leaving little room for long-term strategic planning. National development plans or those concerning a country's education system do not include refugee education. In addition, refugees' educational access and attainment are rarely tracked through national monitoring systems. As a result, refugee children and youth are not only disadvantaged but their schooling needs, as well as achievements, also remain largely invisible.

The recent United Nations High Commissioner for Refugees (UNHCR 2016a) report entitled *Missing Out: Refugee Education in Crisis* has documented a number of realities concerning the refugees' plight, and the difficulties of governments trying to care for them. Firstly, the majority of the world's refugees – 86 percent – are actually living in the world's still-developing regions, with more than a quarter situated in the world's least developed countries. In fact, more than half of the world's refugee children out of school are found in only seven countries: Chad, Democratic Ethiopia, Kenya, Republic of the Congo, Lebanon, Pakistan and Turkey (UNHCR, 2016a, p. 4). Secondly, refugees often live in regions where governments are already experiencing problems in the education of their own children. Those governments face the additional burden of finding school places, trained teachers and learning materials for tens or even hundreds of thousands of newcomers, who often do not speak the language of instruction, and furthermore have lost on average three to four years of schooling (UNHCR, 2016a, p. 4).

By the end of 2015, 6.7 million refugees had been trapped in forced displacement for such long periods that they found themselves living in a protracted state of limbo. Despite the efforts being made to expand the provision of education to more refugee children and youth, the sheer weight of numbers has meant that rates of enrolment in school have declined in the past few years, even in countries where determined efforts have been made to get more refugee children into school (UNHCR, 2016a, p. 5). At the end of 2015, about half of all refugees were children; their learning needs should have been addressed urgently and the impact of their forced displacement should have been minimised as much as possible, but for a great many these possibilities of education have not been forthcoming. The total number of unaccompanied or separated children who applied for asylum worldwide virtually tripled to 98,400 during 2015, compared to 34,300 in 2014. This was the first time that UNHCR had documented such a large number of these claims within a single year since the agency started systematically collecting this type of information in 2006 (UNHCR, 2016b, p. 8). Much of this rise in numbers was linked to the overall increase in asylum applications, yet the proportion of unaccompanied or separated children among all asylum applications rose noticeably from just over 2 percent in 2013 to nearly 5 percent in 2015 (UNHCR, 2016b, p. 44). Worldwide the numbers of refugee families and children with educational and subsistence needs have been increasing relentlessly.

This book focuses on a particular 'subset' of the world's refugee population, Syrian children, and specifically, those who were accepted as refugees into Sweden and Australia. It is concerned with exploring the differences and similarities in the education opportunities provided for these children in both countries. Both are rich, 'first-world' countries that have the capacity and resources to offer education and subsequently employment possibilities to the next generations of adults from Syrian refugee families. While the main objective of this book is to explain the situation regarding the education of refugee children and their families in Australia and Sweden, it also takes into account what is happening in other countries that accept refugees, yet due to their own economic circumstances can barely afford to do so, for example, Lebanon and Bangladesh.

Syrian refugee children

The Syrian refugee crisis has reached catastrophic proportions since the uprising that began in early 2011 against the authoritarian Assad regime. The destruction and havoc wreaked throughout the country resulted in more than 5.4 million Syrians fleeing the country to neighbouring states, i.e. Lebanon, Turkey and Jordan. The conflict in the Syrian Arab Republic – compounded by an ongoing insurgency in Iraq – have also contributed significantly to the rising global number of displaced people. Syria's civil war has created one of the largest and most complex humanitarian crises of our time, and from the start of the civil war in 2011 to September 2015, half of Syria's population of 23 million was displaced, with at least 7.6 million displaced internally and 5 million refugees (Culbertson and Constant, 2015, p. 1). To quote Sirin and Rogers-Sirin (2015, p. 5) at length:

> There are more refugees coming out of Syria than any other nation. Estimates from September 2015 suggest that just over 2 million children have fled Syria

and are living as refugees in neighbouring countries in the Middle East, or North Africa; nearly 11,000 children crossed the Syrian border on their own, and more than 140,000 were born as refugees ... The United Nations and a number of charity organizations provide humanitarian assistance in the form of food, shelter, and medical aid, but the sheer numbers of refugees and funding shortfalls make it difficult to meet even their most urgent needs. Amid deteriorating conditions in countries of first asylum, growing numbers of Syrians have sought protection outside the region. Though many countries have increased the number of refugees they will accept through resettlement, family reunification, emergency scholarship, and humanitarian admission programs, demand far outstrips supply.

This makes the Syrian refugees the world's second-largest refugee population, after the nearly 5 million Palestinian refugees (Nebehay, 2015).

By the end of 2015 there were nearly 5.4 million Syrian refugees worldwide, representing an increase of 1 million men, women and children within a year. The vast majority of these newly displaced Syrians were registered in Turkey (946,800 individuals). Subsequently, Turkey was home to the world's largest refugee population – some 2.54 million people, mostly from the Syrian Arab Republic (UNHCR, 2016b, p. 7). The presence of such large numbers of refugees has made huge demands on overstretched public-sector services, agencies and departments, triggering serious tensions in countries like Turkey and Lebanon with their own development and stability challenges. It has caused crowding in schools and hospitals; rents have risen in poorer areas; downward pressures exist on wages and unemployment worsens in economies already experiencing high joblessness. The public sector in such receiving countries lacks required resources, and their education, health and other services cannot keep pace. Government budgets and infrastructure are increasingly burdened, while funding from the international community cannot in any meaningful way cover the expenses incurred. In communities that are most affected by a significant refugee presence, direct tensions can arise between host-country nationals and Syrians, causing concerns for security and social cohesion (Culbertson and Constant, 2015, p. ix; Carlier, 2018, pp. 1–2). Currently, many refugees still continue to search for safety and refuge in developed countries including Germany, the United Kingdom, Sweden, Australia, Canada and the United States.

When conflict and/or violence erupts in a country, the consequences for its hitherto effective and established educational systems can be devastating. The violence in Syria provides a very relevant example here. Nearly a decade ago, in 2009, 94 percent of the country's children attended primary and lower-secondary education, yet by June 2016 this figure had fallen to 60 percent, leaving 2.1 million children and adolescents with no access to schooling. In neighbouring countries, more than 4.8 million Syrian refugees are registered with the UNHCR, among them approximately 35 percent of school age. In Turkey, with reference to primary and secondary education, only 39 percent of school-aged refugee children and adolescents were enrolled; the figures in Lebanon and Jordan were 40 and 70 percent, respectively. This means that in 2016 nearly 900,000 Syrian school-age refugee children and adolescents were not in school (UNHCR, 2016a, p. 11).

With above 5.6 million registered Syrian refugees, over 2.5 million children are on the run living as refugees and seeking asylum in distant refugee-receiving countries in order to survive (UNICEF, 2019). More than 8.4 million children of war, inside and outside Syria, desperately need humanitarian aid and assistance, as well as the opportunity for education. Responses from neighbouring and distant countries have been wide ranging, particularly to refugee children who fled war-torn Syria. In March 2018 it was reported that more than 40 percent of Syrian refugee children living in neighbouring countries were not being educated, with this number rising due to lack of funding and bullying in schools. This claim was made by the organisation KidsRights, which also stated that despite world leaders agreeing at a 2016 conference to enrol all Syrian refugee children into school by late 2017, 43 percent of Syrian children in Lebanon, Jordan, Egypt, Turkey and Iraq did not have access to an education. Approximately 777,000 of 1.8 million registered Syrian children in the five countries had not been educated at the end of 2017 – which meant nearly 250,000 more out of school than in 2016 (Reuters, 2018).

One Syrian refugee child's story highlights the terror of having to simply survive. Briefly, 13-year-old Mounir (not his real name) fled to Lebanon with his family after surviving a rocket strike but he encountered another form of danger on the streets of Tripoli where he sold sweets on the streets until 11pm, earning approximately 12,000 Lebanese pounds ($8) a day. Mounir was subjected to sexual harassment and verbal abuse, people calling him a 'Syrian dog', and his situation reinforces the following salient facts (Kanso, 2018): firstly, Syrian families in Lebanon have no choice but to send their children to work to get the basic needs, which means children are deprived of education; secondly, less than half of Syrian children attend school; thirdly, more than three quarters of the refugees in Lebanon are living below the poverty line and struggling to survive on less than $4 per day; and fourthly, families feel unable to protect their daughters and are marrying them off early instead of sending them to school in many cases to protect them. The incidence of child marriage has in fact doubled among some Syrian refugee communities (Staunton, 2016; Carlier, 2018, pp. 4, 10).

To understand the horrific conditions facing Syrian children displaced by war, but still living in Syria, it has been reported that since the start of 2018, the United Nations (UN) has verified more than 1,200 violations carried out against such children, with more than 600 children maimed or killed, and another 180 recruited for combat purposes. Furthermore the city of Idlib, which is situated in Syria's northwest, is now home to one of the highest numbers of internally displaced children in the country. It is estimated that 1 million children across Idlib are now living in perilous conditions (UNICEF Australia, 2018).

The right to education

Education is associated with economic growth for a country, alleviation of and moving out of conditions of poverty for families, establishment of personal stability and economic empowerment and the creation of better developed and more advanced communities. The first announcement of compulsory primary school education as a universal entitlement occurred in 1948 with the Universal Declaration of Human Rights. Access to a basic human right was also enshrined in the 1951 Refugee Convention (United Nations Human Rights Office of the High Commissioner, n.d.) and the 1989 Convention on the Rights of the Child, which came into force on 2 September 1990. Not only is education a basic human right, it also protects children and youths from enforced recruitment into armed groups, sexual exploitation, child marriage and child labour. More positively, it inspires and empowers refugees to obtain knowledge and the skills required to live productive and independent lives (Culbertson and Constant, 2015, pp. 16–20). Despite all these acknowledged benefits, the education prospects of many refugee children around the world remain bleak. With every new refugee crisis, UN agencies, non-governmental organisations (NGOs) and government agencies stumble or can take only half-measures when it comes to the education of refugees.

In 2018, the UNHCR reported that 68.5 million people were forcibly displaced and half of that number are children under the age of 18. Among them 25.4 million refugees of whom only 4.7 percent were resettled in a few countries and half of them were of school age. Their access to education was limited, with 4 million unable to attend school (UNHCR, 2018). In fact, if those refugees not under UNHCR care are included, by the end of 2017, there were more than 25.4 million refugees worldwide and more than half of the world's refugee population – 52 percent – were below the age of 18 (UNHCR, 2017b, p. 3). One important statistic stood out: among those who fell under the UNHCR's aegis, there are currently 4 million refugee children not in school (UNHCR, 2017a, p. 10). The report published in mid-September 2017 reinforced the seriousness of these statistics and called for education to be a vital component of any humanitarian response. Firstly, more than 4 million refugee children have not had the opportunity to attend school in the previous academic year. Secondly, there were 6.4 million refugees who were of school aged between 5 and 17, among those who fell under the mandate of the Office of the United Nations Commissioner for Refugees. Thirdly, it was evident that as refugee children grew older, the obstacles increased. Just 23 percent of refugee adolescents were enrolled in secondary school, compared to 84 percent of all adolescents globally. Moreover, low-income countries in which the proportion of young people in secondary education was low as 9 percent were hosting 28 percent of the world's refugees (United Nations, 2017).

A school which is free from war and fighting is the first place in which refugee children and young people can start to regain what is very much taken for granted in Western countries: safety, friendship, order and peace. It is evident that refugee students generally have greater education and support requirements than most other newly arrived migrant students. Another factor to consider is that most refugee children and young people have had disrupted or non-existent education prior to their arrival in countries such as Australia and Sweden. Many have no literacy skills in their first language, and have experienced complex physical and mental health problems. Adapting to a new school environment is a major and often traumatic undertaking for refugee children when they arrive in a new country or refugee camp (Hoot, 2011). Yet education is crucial in enabling refugee children to sufficiently adjust psychosocially and be able to enjoy the benefits of cognitive growth (Eisenbruch, 1988). For this reason, it is clearly evident that educators need to be mindful of the needs, obstacles and successful educational pathways for children refugees.

In one recent study (Graham et al., 2016), the authors noted that parents' misunderstandings about educational styles, teachers' low expectations and stereotyping tendencies, students' bullying and racial discrimination, as well as pre- and post-migration trauma, and forced detention can all be regarded as risk factors preventing refugee children's effective learning. Conversely, they also asserted that high academic and life ambitions, parental involvement in education, a supportive home and school environment, teachers' understanding of their students' linguistic and cultural heritage and healthy peer relationships can all contribute to refugee children's success in school.

Why Australia and Sweden?

Both Australia and Sweden are economically, socially and politically well-developed industrial countries with 'welfare state-like' institutions and processes, like Germany, the United Kingdom, Canada and the United States, among others. Australia and Sweden have responded to the Syrian crisis in their own way with features that define refugee children's schooling and trajectories for transition to life and work. Yet, while both Australia and Sweden are advanced, Western economies with liberal democratic systems, and have similar international legal obligations to asylum seekers, it is very evident that Australia has pursued different policies because values inherent in the Refugee Convention have been rejected in favour of alterative political policies. For example, Australia has mandatory detention for refugees where Sweden does not, mainly because of the common refugee policy formulated by the European Union. These serve the interests of politicians who determine policy, and there is currently no countervailing influence in Australian society that is strong enough to support the norms of international law.

Approximately 6,500 refugees are resettled in Australia annually, including adolescent-aged refugees who enter the country's school system. Moreover, a political commitment was made in 2015 to accept 12,000 Syrian refugees, which meant in effect a greater influx of high-need students into the education system (Crealy, 2015, p. 21). Asylum-seeker policy in Australia has been developed in recent times as a response to a purported national security threat, whereas Sweden has not done so. It has a much higher rate of asylum applications and is more accessible geographically than Australia. Studies on comparisons of refugees/asylum seekers in Sweden and Australia have been done (see, for example, Haandrikman and Hassanen, 2014; de Silva, 2017). Over a decade ago, one commentator noted that Sweden and Australia were highly favoured by refugees fleeing Iraq: 'I spoke with Iraqis who queued daily in interminable lines at the UNHCR, hoping to be pre-selected for resettlement to Australia and Sweden, two of the leading countries in Iraqi admission at the time' (Berman, 2015). The intricacies of Australia's acceptance of refugees and humanitarian entrants can be stated here. As of 2015–16, Australia accepted 17,555 refugees in total and this figure included: 6,730 refugees; 5,032 special humanitarian entrants; 2,003 people granted onshore protection visas; 1,277 women deemed to be 'at risk'; and 3,790 people granted visas under the government's commitment to deliver additional humanitarian places to people displaced by the conflicts in Syria and Iraq (Winsor, 2018).

As the chosen case study countries for this book, Australia and Sweden represent a range of diverse responses to schooling refugee Syrian children. Comparison of these two nations is underpinned by wide-ranging themes that involve the educational settings for Syrian refugee children in the two countries. These were investigated in light of the following key areas:

- Australia and Sweden's socio-economic context;
- responses to refugee crises in general and the Syrian refugee crisis in particular;
- education system and related policies that specifically concern the requirements for refugee children to achieve certain competencies and completion;
- national curriculum and course content relating to refugee education and pedagogies of peace and hope;
- the role of teachers, teaching strategies and other existing support structures (school and non-school) for Syrian refugee students;
- Syrian refugees' voices (parents and children) about the schooling offered in the host country.

In order to provide data on the schooling experiences of Syrian refugee children in Australia and Sweden, interviews with individuals or groups were conducted. The responses of refugee children will be critically analysed utilising UNHCR's Education in Emergencies and critical pedagogies, pedagogy of the displaced and pedagogy of peace and hope. Recommendations for refugee education will be developed from an analysis of the refugee children's perspectives.

It is important to note here that Australia and Sweden do share some similarities in their treatment of refugees. Phelps (2013, pp. 45–6) writes that both countries have successfully developed alternatives to detention based on case management in the community. This system entails a trusted individual being responsible for working with migrants to ensure that their practical needs are met, for instance housing, details concerning the migration process, legal advice, etc. This case manager helps the migrant to build a relationship of trust, taking time throughout the immigration process to explore all potential long-term options, including leave to remain, assisted return and possibilities in third countries. The origins of such case-management programmes are significant, being introduced as reactions to systemic crises. In Sweden, change followed a public and media outcry over conditions in the late 1990s. For Australia, international condemnation of the mandatory indefinite detention of children and adults combined with flagrant errors such as the repeated deportations of Australian citizens forced the government to introduce radical community-based programmes for irregular migrants arriving on Australian territory. It is therefore evident that in Australia and Sweden, case management has become an established part of the immigration system.

Organisation of this book

The introduction to the book has discussed the background to the ongoing Syrian refugee crisis, the growing numbers of refugees fleeing the country and why Australia and Sweden were chosen as the case studies. The actual study focus – Syrian refugee children – was explained and justified in more detail and what could be achieved by investigating their experiences and perspectives. The global response to the Syrian crisis has also been discussed so that the current initiatives of global agencies and the rest of the world are understood. With the crisis in Syria and displacement of people to neighbouring countries and elsewhere in the world, issues of 'moral panic' and 'Islamophobia' have occurred alongside humanitarian responses offered by neighbouring countries such as Lebanon, global agencies like the UNHCR and developed countries.

Chapter 2 critically examines the selected models of educational response/ intervention for refugee children. One theory points to a modified version of segmented assimilation, a popular model of immigrant integration to the host society. The model identifies factors that allow immigrants to 'melt' into the host country's dominant culture. The theory emphasises the role of schools in encouraging successful assimilation of immigrants, particularly refugees. This theory, however, has serious limitations and criticisms of it will be discussed in this chapter. Education in emergencies is another model of education for children in emergency situations such as wars. It was developed as early as 1949 with the establishment of the United Nations Relief and Works Agency for Palestine refugees. Based on this model, resources were developed by a team of experts in 2000 and have since been edited and extended (Sinclair, 2001). Principles from this model have been utilised in this book. Finally, in examining models of refugee education, the critical pedagogy of Paulo Freire, as reflected in a pedagogy of the displaced (Maadad and Rodwell,

2017), and pedagogies of peace and hope have been included in a new framework for analysing and evaluating the refugee education provisions of Sweden and Australia.

Chapter 3 describes the methodology used in this study and also in the contexts of the two countries and their education systems. Chapters 4 and 5 describe and explain Syrian refugee children's schooling experiences in Australia and Sweden, respectively. Both chapters present the following key topics: socio-economic context; response to refugee crises and the Syrian experience in particular; the education system and policies relating to refugees and requirements for achieving certain competencies and levels of completion; national curriculum and course content relating to refugee education and pedagogies of peace and hope; role of teachers, teaching strategies and other existing support structures (for example, school and non-school) for Syrian refugee students; and Syrian refugee children's voices about their schooling. Chapter 6 encapsulates a detailed cross-country comparison of Sweden and Australia, with an emphasis on how education for Syrian refugee children was conceptualised and implemented with their 'voices' reported here; reference is made to other studies as well. Finally, the concluding chapter, Chapter 7, articulates the lessons learnt about Syrian refugee children's education in Australia and Sweden, with useful effective recommendations being made on how and why their refugee education systems should be improved, and what such improvements should achieve.

This book was about those who needed to be accorded a chance of survival and hope in a foreign country in circumstances not of their making. What was happening to refugee children and their families? What experiences and challenges did they encounter? The book aimed to investigate the perspectives of children, their parents, teachers and community leaders, with specific reference to the educational and survival enhancement opportunities for children, parents and the host community in all three chosen countries. Examined here were the salient features of Syrian refugee children's schooling and trajectories for transition to life and employment in two distant worlds apart and host countries, that may be characterised as welfare states (even though the actual welfare apparatuses are being gradually dismantled or changed, given that 'free market' economic policies increasingly dominate). Our comparison of Australia and Sweden entailed an explanation and description of wide-ranging themes concerning the Syrian refugee crisis, and refugee children's education. These included – but were not limited to – disrupted education, displacement from home and country, socio-economic dispossession/dislocation, global response to the refugee crisis, nation-state response to the Syrian refugee crisis, education policies and provisions of host countries as they apply to refugee children, and principles of pedagogies of peace and hope.

Critically, this book focused on the perspectives of Syrian refugee children and their voiced experiences. Their voices were central to the analysis for the main reason that their viewpoints could contribute in a practical way to the development of pedagogical approaches that would support their schooling and an effective and productive transition to life in the host countries. Furthermore, the opinions, suggestions and experiences of other stakeholders such as parents, caregivers, teachers and school and state officials were included for greater understanding so that as many relevant contexts are covered. An equally important objective of this book was to elicit recommendations for educational practices and content as informed by Syrian refugee children. The recommendations for refugee education that were proposed here will be useful for teachers directly engaged in educating refugee students and this could positively impact on young refugee students finding their way to a new and better life.

It is envisaged that while this book provided a snapshot of the times, i.e. the Syrian refugee students' experiences of schooling following an exodus from war-torn Syria, it will remain as up to date as possible as the data are gathered. Writing this book has meant keeping up with the news, reports, statistics, stories, anecdotes, etc. regarding the Syrian refugee population and especially what is happening to the children. Thus the analysis has to have currency and will be updated as necessary. The methodology and framework of analysis will therefore not become easily obsolete or the findings outdated; they can be utilised for future studies.

It is hoped that the readers of this book will agree that the rewards of investing in education for all children are immense and far-reaching. There is solid evidence that quality education gives children a place of safety and helps eradicate the horrors of child marriage, child labour, children fighting as soldiers, exploitative and dangerous work and teenage pregnancy. Properly targeted education will give refugee children the opportunity to make friends and find mentors, and provide them with the necessary skills for self-reliance, problem solving, collaborative teamwork and critical thinking. It improves their job prospects and boosts confidence and self-esteem. Given the numbers of Syrian refugee children who are currently not receiving formal education, the strained capacities of host countries, the political considerations and the risks posed to children and society at large, this tragic situation must be alleviated through the development and implementation of innovative and effective educational strategies. Efforts need to be coordinated, knowledge shared, evidence-based decisions made, efficiency improved and resources solicited.

References

Berman, Chantal E. (2015). 'Resettling Syrian Refugees: Lessons from the (Forgotten) Iraqi Refugee Crisis'. *Brookings*, 24 September. Retrieved 23 October 2018 from www.brookings.edu/blog/markaz/2015/09/24/resettling-syrian-refugees-lessons-from-the-forgotten-iraqi-refugee-crisis/.

Carlier, Wannes (2018). *Background Report: The Widening Educational Gap for Syrian Refugee Children*. Amsterdam: KidsRights Foundation.

Crealy, Isobel Rose (2015). The Peter Mitchell Churchill Fellowship to Investigate Language and Cultural Inclusion Programs Illustrating Best Practice in the Integration of Adolescent Refugee Students – Canada, USA. The Winston Churchill Memorial Trust of Australia.

Culbertson, Shelly and Constant, Louay (2015). *Education of Syrian Refugee Children: Managing the Crisis in Turkey, Lebanon, and Jordan*. Santa Monica, CA: RAND Corporation.

De Silva, Mary Lynn (2017). Norm Circles, Stigma and the Securitization of Asylum: A Comparative Study of Australia and Sweden. PhD thesis, University of Western Australia.

Educate a Child (n.d.). 'Refugees'. Retrieved 12 October 2018 from https://educateachild.org/explore/barriers-to-education/refugees.

Eisenbruch, Maurice (1988). 'The Mental Health of Refugee Children and Their Cultural Development'. *International Migration Review*, 22, 282–300.

Graham, Hamish R., Minhas, Ripudaman S. and Paxton, Georgia (2016). 'Learning Problems in Children of Refugee Background: A Systematic Review'. *Pediatrics*, 137(6), e20153994.

Haandrikman, Karen and Hassanen, Sadia (2014). 'Onward Migration of African Europeans: Comparing Attitudes to Migration Motives'. *Stockholm Research Reports in Demography*, Vol. 15. Stockholm University, Department of Sociology, Demography Unit.

Hoot, James L. (2011). 'Working with Very Young Refugee Children in Our Schools: Implications for the World's Teachers'. *Procedia: Social and Behavioral Sciences*, 15, 1751–1755.

Kanso, Herba (2018). 'Poverty Forces Syrian Refugee Children into Work'. *Thomson Reuters Foundation, Reliefweb*, 12 June. Retrieved 24 October 2018 from https://reliefweb.int/report/lebanon/poverty-forces-syrian-refugee-children-work.

Loprinzi, Siena (2016). Refugee Policies and the Interactions of the United Nations and European Union. Honours thesis, Portland State University.

Maadad, N. and Rodwell, G. (2017). *Schooling and Education in Lebanon for Syrian and Palestinian Refugees inside and outside the Camps*. Bern: Peter Lang.

Nebehay, Stephanie (2015). 'Syrians Largest Refugee Group after Palestinians: UN'. *Reuters*, 15 January. Retrieved 24 October 2018 from www.reuters.com/article/2015/01/07/us-mideast-crisis-syria-refugees-idUSKBN0KG0AZ20150107.

Phelps, Jerome (2013). 'Alternatives to Detention in the UK: From Enforcement to Engagement?' *Forced Migration Review*, no. 44, pp. 45–48. Retrieved 23 October 2018 from www.refworld.org/pdfid/523bf00b4.pdf.

Reuters (2018). 'Report: Fears Rise of "Lost Generation" as More Syrian Refugee Children out of School'. *VOA News*, 27 March. Retrieved 24 October 2018 from www.voanews.com/a/syrian-refugees-lacking-education/4320249.html.

Sinclair, M. (2001). 'Education in Emergencies'. In J. Crisp, C. Talbot, and D. B. Cipollone (eds), *Learning for a Future: Refugee Education in Developing Countries* (pp. 1–84). Lausanne: United Nations Publications.

Sirin, Selcuk R. and Rogers-Sirin, Lauren (2015). *The Educational and Mental Health Needs of Syrian Refugee Children*. Washington, DC: Migration Policy Institute.

Staunton, Marie (2016). 'Why Education for Refugee Children Is a Matter of Human Rights AND the Right Thing to Do'. *Crown Agents*, 18 March. Retrieved 24 October 2018 from https://medium.com/@crownagents/why-education-for-refugee-children-is-a-matter-of-human-rights-and-the-right-thing-to-do-35f1b70f38c4.

UNHCR (1994). *Refugee Children: Guidelines on Protection and Care*. Geneva: United Nations High Commissioner for Refugees.

UNHCR (2016a). *Missing Out: Refugee Education in Crisis*. Geneva. Retrieved 24 October 2018 from www.unhcr.org/57d9d01d0.

UNHCR (2016b). *Global Trends: Forced Displacement in 2015*. Geneva. Retrieved 24 October 2018 from www.unhcr.org/statistics/unhcrstats/576408cd7/unhcr-global-trends-2015.html.

UNHCR (2017a). *Turn the Tide: Refugee Education in Crisis*. Geneva. Retrieved 12 October 2018 from www.unhcr.org/5b852f8e4.pdf.

UNHCR (2017b). *Global Trends: Forced Displacement in 2017*. Geneva. Retrieved 20 February 2019 from www.unhcr.org/5b27be547.pdf.

UNHCR (2018). *Figures at a Glance*. Retrieved 21 February 2019 from www.unhcr.org/figures-at-a-glance.html.

UNICEF (2019). 'Syria Emergency'. Retrieved 22 February 2019 from www.unicef.org/appeals/syrianrefugees.html.

UNICEF (n.d.). 'Fact Sheet: A Summary of the Rights under the Convention on the Rights of the Child'. Retrieved 23 October 2018 from www.unicef.org/crc/files/Rights_overview.pdf.

UNICEF Australia (2018). 'Syria Crisis Appeal'. Retrieved 24 October 2018 from www.unicef.org.au/appeals/syria-crisis-appeal.

United Nations (2017). 'Over 3.5 Million Refugee Children Missing Out on Education, UN Report Finds'. Sustainable Development Goals, 13 September. Retrieved 23 October from www.un.org/sustainabledevelopment/blog/2017/09/over-3-5-million-refugee-children-missing-out-on-education-un-report-finds/.

United Nations Human Rights Office of the High Commissioner (n.d.). Convention on the Rights of the Child. Retrieved 12 October 2018 from www.ohchr.org/en/professionalinterest/pages/crc.aspx.

Winsor, Morgan (2018). 'On World Refugee Day 2018, a Record 68.5 Million Forcibly Displaced Last Year'. *ABC News*, 21 June. Retrieved 25 February 2019 from https://abcnews.go.com/International/world-refugee-day-2018-record-685-million-forcibly/story?id=56026315.

2
MAKING EDUCATION AVAILABLE TO REFUGEE CHILDREN

Innovative theories and effective practices

Introduction

The situation concerning Syrian and Myanmar children refugees from a theoretical perspective dominates this chapter, given that their travails have been the subject of much international news reporting over the last two years. Most readers will understand that the dreadful plight of the refugee child befalls other refugee children in a hundred or more countries in South and Central America, throughout Southeast Asia and in fact most of Asia, a host of African countries and throughout the Middle East. This is a tragic story of traumatised young people, many without parents or carers, or mature siblings. What most have in common is trauma, and for most – even if held latently – a desire to have some kind of education, with a distant opportunity of taking up a new life in a host country in some far off land.

As wave after wave of refugees challenge existing border security laws, oblivious to the political upheavals in developed Western countries, the need for the education and schooling of refugee children in these nations has prompted governments to rethink their relevant school education policies. It has meant that old theories of assimilation need to be changed in the face of enrolments of traumatised refugee children. Issues of mental health assume new dimensions in school educational policy as it emerges in many local level reports (Sirin and Rogers-Sirin, 2015) that refugee students' psychological traumas need to be dealt with because they are increasing at an almost exponential rate and becoming a serious block to learning. Schools and teachers in many countries are finding themselves under pressure from new challenges associated with teaching traumatised refugee students in their classrooms.

As if to throw additional fuel onto this fire, however, national and/or regional governments and school education authorities encounter additional challenges from the attitudes of the surrounding community, often in the form of needing to manage or curtail 'moral panic'-inspired anti-immigration views or assumptions. In Australia and especially since 9/11 the chief example of this has been Islamophobia, a widespread suspicion of refugees and asylum seekers from predominantly Muslim countries who are perceived as not wanting to 'fit in'. Such feelings are whipped up by ultra-conservative politicians and compliant media outlets, not to mention an at-times hostile and vitriolic social media landscape, in the form of 'tweets' on issues that generate their own momentum. Notwithstanding the everyday politics that consume certain countries' refugee and asylum-seeker policies and regulations, educational theorists, education department heads and teachers have been striving to develop new strategies to ameliorate the situation of traumatised refugee students. This chapter seeks to explore two seminal texts on education that provided a theoretical critique of what education should really be about. The first is Paulo Freire's *Pedagogy of the Oppressed*, originally published in Portuguese in 1968 and translated by Myra Ramos into English in 1970. One of Freire's central tenets was the belief that 'education is freedom' which can lead individuals to true liberation, while the 'banking' concept of education – one in which students are simply empty vessels to be filled – is in fact an instrument of oppression (Barmania, 2011). The second is Augusto Boal's *Theatre of the Oppressed*, a philosophy first elaborated during the 1970s where theatre served as a means of promoting social and political change and justice through the actions of the audience. Influenced by Paulo Freire, Boal set out to work for social and political activism, to resolve conflicts and build communities (Mandala Centre for Change, n.d.), using theatrical games and techniques to examine and unpack the dynamics of oppressing the poor, the powerless and the refugee.

Inspired by Freire's philosophy, this book advances the concept of the pedagogy of the displaced, which views the disadvantaged situation of children from refugee backgrounds as socially constructed and argues that the dehumanising effect of war has been responsible for their displaced status and their subjection to a state of 'oppression'. Their oppressors, whether at the micro or macro level, are those who exert power over them, whether active or passive. Passive oppressors are those who support the actions of active oppressors or fail to take action to help those oppressed (Boal, 1985). In the case of refugees, active oppressors may include privileged individuals, dominant groups and institutions (government or otherwise) that directly wield power over refugees in host countries.

The challenge to make schooling available

At the most basic level, the problem has been how to make places for learning available to so many displaced refugee children that have fled from war-torn Syria. Some very innovative and quite different approaches have been developed to deal with this underlying problem. Two of them are discussed below.

Making schools available in Lebanon

Writing in the *Guardian* on 13 January 2016, former United Kingdom prime minister Gordon Brown wrote of what some governments were doing to alleviate the alienation, hopelessness and educational shortcomings experienced by refugee children in Lebanon. 'Amid the Syrian chaos of carnage, starvation and evacuation, there is a tiny glimmer of hope' in the fact that the 'Lebanese government has declared that it has taken 207,000 Syrian refugee children off the streets and given them places in their country's public schools' (Brown, 2016). This was being achieved through the Lebanese government funding 'double-shift' schools. For Brown, however, it was 'imperative that money is found to give all young refugees the hope that education provides'.

It was the introduction of the 'double-shift school system' that unlocked the opportunity for hundreds of thousands of extra school places in Lebanon to be made available to Syrian refugee children. Local Lebanese children are educated in the morning in their neighbourhood schools but the same classrooms are now being made available to refugee children in the afternoon and early evenings. This was good news for the hundreds of thousands of Syrian refugee children throughout the country. Because the double-shift system used existing schools, avoiding the huge capital costs and virtual impossibility of building new ones, the average cost was just $10 per school place per week. Some schools can accommodate up to 700 refugee students in the afternoons. According to Panella (2016), of the 259 schools offering double-shift education, 85,000 children were at that time enrolled. One recent example of this was reported in 2018 (Cherri and Hariri, 2018). Bar Elias School in Lebanon's Bekaa Valley is one of 350 that operates a 'second shift' where essentially two school days are fit into one; 770 Syrian pupils attend the afternoon shift in classes of approximately 35 and the curriculum, teaching materials and most of the teachers are in fact the same as those of the Lebanese children attending the morning lessons (Cherri and Hariri, 2018).

At the time of Brown's article in the *Guardian* there were 'robust plans to offer 400,000 places by doubling the number of schools'. Moreover, other Middle Eastern countries were taking up the challenge to alleviate the dire plight of Syrian refugee children. Brown claimed that 'as a direct result of Lebanon's success, Turkey and Jordan are now ready to make double-shift schools the centrepiece of this year's educational efforts for refugees' (Brown, 2016; see also Culbertson et al., 2016). Working with United Nations International Children's Emergency Fund (UNICEF), Turkey was reported as planning to double its school places for refugees to more than 450,000 during 2016. Meanwhile, at the same time 'in Jordan, where just over 100,000 refugees are already in school, the aim is to double places' (Brown, 2016).

Apart from the loss of their school educational opportunities, the human suffering of these young people has become intolerable and inhumane. According to Brown (2016):

as more and more girls and boys arrive from Syria on the streets of Lebanon, Jordan and Turkey, disturbing new statistics show rates of child marriage among refugee girls have doubled from 12% to 26%, and child labour among out-of-school boys and girls is rapidly worsening. One recent survey estimates that a third of boys and girls displaced from their home country have become labourers, often working illegally in unsafe conditions.

During the first five years of the terrible Syrian civil war, without the provision of education, refugee parents had to choose between leaving the Middle East region altogether, or taking the perilous sea voyage across the Mediterranean to Europe. These were the so-called 'death voyages' (Williams, 2015), where in the eastern Mediterranean alone several boats carried Syrians arriving directly from Lebanon to Cyprus in 2018, thereby complicating the capacity of the asylum system to cope with refugees' homelessness and simply process their reception and shelter needs (UNHCR, 2019, p. 11). By 2016, there were an estimated 2 million Syrian child refugees scattered around the world. Tragically, some of them, having witnessed unspeakable terror in their home country, bear appalling scars of trauma, perhaps indelibly affecting their ability to participate in schooling of the kind described above.

According to Brown (2016), it is 'well known that the offer of education is the most important factor in giving previously demoralised young people hope that there is a future worth preparing for'. Those Syrian refugee children who attended the 'double-shift' schools had the advantage of learning in proper school buildings, with trained teachers. However, because Arabic is not the language of instruction in Lebanese schools, they faced the hurdle of gaining literacy in another language, if they wished to progress in their learning. Brown's 2016 article, affirming the positive and healing role of education, was published at a time when people thought that circumstances could not get worse. Then the tragedy of Myanmar/Bangladesh, which erupted in August 2017, came to the world's attention.

Creating educational spaces in refugee camps in Bangladesh

The immediate cause of the refugee crisis in Myanmar was the launching of a security operation by the country's armed forces in the north of Rakhine State. It drove thousands of Rohingya children, women and men to flee over the border into Bangladesh in search of safety. According to Eleanor Albert (2018), the Rohingya ethnic group was primarily Muslim and made up approximately one third of the state's population. They lived in a predominantly Buddhist country which had discriminated against them since the late 1970s. Since independence in 1948, successive governments in Myanmar had refuted the Rohingya's historical claims to citizenship and denied the group recognition as one of its 135 ethnic groups. Instead, the Rohingya were deemed to be illegal immigrants from Bangladesh, despite the fact many traced their roots in Myanmar back through the centuries (Albert, 2018; Calamur, 2017).

As stories of violence against women and children and horrific images were documented in the international mainstream media and social media – villages burned, infants thrown in rivers, babies and mothers shot – and prolific accounts from makeshift camps in neighbouring Bangladesh, where survivors were struggling to find clean water, food and proper shelter, concerned observers reeled in shock. Increasingly, researchers and international authorities demanded more psychological assistance for these young people (Theirworld, 2017). Young people, perhaps, vulnerable in any culture during the most settled of times, were being 'exposed to trauma on an extreme scale in what UN human rights spokesman Zeid Ra'ad Al Hussein called 'textbook ethnic cleansing' in western Myanmar' (Theirworld, 2017).

According to Fatema Khyrunnar, a child protection officer for UNICEF and helping to establish child-friendly spaces in the camps, 'these children have been through a terrible experience. They are heavily traumatised.' Furthermore, it was reported that when they were exposed to periods of prolonged fear, chronic neglect or abuse, poverty and hunger, children's stress responses would go into overdrive with devastating consequences (Theirworld, 2017). More than 18,000 children were reported to have received help through the child-friendly spaces since August, 2017 (Save the Children, 2018, p. 9). Many more, however, still needed comfort and counselling.

By November 2017 the number of Myanmar refugees escaping into Bangladesh were in excess of 600,000. The conditions from which they were escaping were vividly shown in the drawings of Rohingya children, depicting helicopter massacres of villages, tragically on Armistice Day 2017. ABC News (Australia) reported the efforts made to help these children in Bangladesh refugee camps:

> In the refugee camps of Bangladesh, a small handful of psychologists are attempting the near impossible — trying to counsel hundreds of thousands of traumatised Rohingya refugees …
> Alongside mothers who have lost children, [their] patients also include children with no parents.
> 'A few of the children, they don't have any parents, any relatives,' [one psychologist said].
> 'They have been experiencing – they have seen in front of them – father and mother both slaughtered or burned.' …
> The images are confronting – helicopters, shooting down from above, burning villages, and people fleeing in boats …
> A quarter of young children are malnourished and the disease threat hangs like an ominous cloud.
> *(Bennett, 2017)*

The Rohingya refugee children comprised 50 percent of the entire refugee population and were living in highly crowded environments (approx. 8 m^2/person), where they were susceptible to malnutrition and disease. As well as the everyday stresses of displacement, these children had endured astonishing trauma, with little or no access to safe facilities, and at the mercy of serious risks to their protection, including child marriage, child labour, trafficking and abuse (Children on the Edge, 2018). One educational solution, developed by the Children on the Edge organisation in association with UNICEF, was the founding of the 'Rohingya Children's Programme'.

The result was the building of 45 small classrooms, dispersed throughout the unofficial refugee camp on the Bangladesh/Myanmar border. Classrooms were erected out of mud, either within or alongside existing abodes. As many as 45 Rohingya refugees from the camps received training as teachers through a 'train the trainer' programme. In their charge were 2,700 children who in this way were given the opportunity to learn in their own language and culture. Whether this gave them the opportunity to learn about living in their host country, Bangladesh, is not clear. However, this project was based on local partnership and active participation of the refugee community. Subsequently, children, parents and the wider community were engaged at all levels, and staff worked with parents to increase their comprehension of the importance of education and to encourage them in supporting various aspects of their children's learning (Smitheram, 2017).

'As never before': The need for the education and schooling of refugee children

As refugee children are scattered around the Western world, and eventually are accommodated in various countries' particular education systems, observers are recognising that all bring with them varying levels of trauma. In short, each tide of refugees experiences a different kind of trauma. For example, in comparing refugee children from the Second Gulf War (2003–11) who are in Detroit schools with the earlier presence of children from the Lebanese Civil War (1975–90), Walbridge and Aziz (2000, p. 339) commented:

> chemicals [were] used in warfare and/or [they were] from deplorable conditions in the refugee camps where they lived for months or years after they rose up against Saddam Hussein at the end of the Gulf War. Having believed American promises that they would be assisted by the Allied Forces, but then abandoned, they carry with them the bitterness at the betrayal of the American government as well as the fear that Saddam will still retaliate against them …
>
> Children of the Iraqi refugee community are challenging teachers and the school system as never before. Reports coming out of the schools are substantially different from those when the schools were trying to integrate Lebanese children. While Lebanese children had seen war and suffering and

did pose problems, the trauma suffered by Iraqi children appears to have been of a far greater magnitude.

Consequently, it was experiences such as the above which caused educational theorists to ask 'what are the school educational needs of refugee children?' Are there any generalities or theories which can be applied? Of course, this referred to settings such as those in the provision of refugee camps in host countries such as Lebanon, and as described above by Brown (2016), and the schools of Detroit, Michigan as described by Walbridge and Aziz (2000).

Paulo Freire's *Pedagogy of the Oppressed* as a theory for educating refugee children

With massive international sales and often considered to be a foundational text of critical paradigms, Paulo Freire's *Pedagogy of the Oppressed* (1996 [1968]) proposed an educational theory of learning that articulated a new relationship between teacher, learner and society, where the learners were among the powerless and oppressed groups in society. As a critical paradigm, it was rooted in historical realism that recognised not one, but multiple realties, which were socially constructed and shaped by social, political, cultural, economic, ethnic and gender values (Guba and Lincoln, 1994; Scotland, 2012).

Freire's pedagogical theory proved to be very influential, particularly during the more radical late 1960s and early 1970s, when Marxist-inspired ideologies and interpretations of the history of school education and what education should actually set out to do were highly popular. Dedicated to people and/or communities perceived to be oppressed, the book was based on Freire's own experience in helping Brazilian adults in urban slums to read and write, and his efforts to incorporate into their learning shared discussion of their experiences related to the words in which they were becoming literate. Freire included a detailed Marxist class analysis in his exploration of the educational relationship between the coloniser and the colonised, between the poor slum worker and the rich and powerful business owners who employed him/her at the lowest possible wages.

Freire (1996 [1968]) contended that traditional pedagogy represented a 'banking model of education', because it treated the student like a child's piggy bank, as an empty vessel to be filled with the knowledge that those in power wanted him/her to know. A central thesis of the pedagogy of the oppressed was that the perceived ignorance and lethargy of the poor resulted from their domination economically, socially and politically by the powerful elites in society. Freire argued that in some countries the oppressors used the education and political systems to maintain a 'culture of silence'. Instead, Freire argued for a pedagogy that treated learners as co-creators of knowledge that was grounded in life as they experienced it. This approach enabled students, who were learning to read and write the sounds they could speak, to increase their understanding of their own situation and realise how they could act to change it. As a result of his own teaching experiences, Freire contended that the oppressed can be liberated through an enlightened pedagogy, avoiding authoritarian, structured, hierarchical teacher–pupil models and basing learning on the actual experiences of students, as well as continual shared interaction and questioning.

This pedagogy of hope that Freire (1995) expounded has the potential to transform the world not only of those living in the urban slums of Brazil, but also the world of refugee children. This possibility was not to be taken as light-hearted illusion or light-headed foolishness. He maintained that hope, as an ontological need, must be at the heart of what all the progressive educator does, as an impetus for transformative action. Freire's critical pedagogy can be seen as thoroughly informing a pedagogy of peace in so far as hope is the energy for transformation, while peace is its by-product. No matter how impoverished or illiterate, learners can develop a new awareness of self and their place in the world, gain literacy, learn how to exercise the right to be heard and how to work towards a transformed life. Freire used the term 'conscientization' to describe the new level of critical consciousness that oppressed learners gained from such learning.

Freire's pedagogical theory was grounded in the actual realities of students' lives, but dependent on teachers' interactions with students in making them aware of future possibilities. Applied to the education of refugee children, this interpretation suggests that there are two levels of teaching and learning which should be considered. The first is the short-term present-oriented response to the immediate learning needs of the refugee students, such as dealing with psychological trauma, finding out levels of literacy and education already achieved and learning the basic new knowledge needed for survival in the host country. The second level is the longer-term future-oriented response of providing the inspiration, knowledge and practical learning pathways for refugee students to pursue their own envisaged futures.

Responding to refugee students' immediate needs

In trying to deal effectively with the immediate needs of refugee students, teachers have developed innovative approaches to learning which can help students to deal with the trauma they have faced. Some of them have drawn inspiration from the arts and the healing power of involvement in music, the visual arts and drama. The theatrical work of Augusto Boal has proved to be invaluable in many contexts.

Adapting Augusto Boal's Theatre of the Oppressed for refugee children

The Brazilian theatre practitioner Augusto Boal's (1985) *Theatre of the Oppressed*, first elaborated in the 1970s in Brazil and later in Europe, described theatrical forms that can be used in classrooms to liberate 'the oppressed'. Influenced by Freire's pedagogy, Boal's techniques used classroom-based theatre as a means of promoting social and political change; in Brazil this involved response to an oppressive military dictatorship, and dealing primarily with issues of persecution and discrimination. Boal's concept subsequently became valued as a therapeutic educational method. In the *Theatre of the Oppressed*, the initially spectator audience becomes active, whereby as 'spect-actors' they explore, show, analyse and transform the reality in which they are living. This approach has proved effective in helping refugee students to overcome the trauma of their experiences.

Dealing with refugee students' psychological trauma

Critically for the major themes that are investigated in this book, Sinclair's (2001) research centred on education for refugee children before their resettlement in other countries. It revealed a major need for successful adjustment: 'meeting the psychological and social needs of stressed and traumatized children through education' (p. 1). For Sinclair 'the psychosocial wellbeing of refugee students … includes a sense of safety, a sense of self, and an adjustment to the cultural expectations of a new country while maintaining a connection to their heritage' (p. 1). In her survey of educational responses designed for emergency situations, Sinclair contended that school education should be viewed as an essential element of humanitarian response to crisis. However, this idea was not without some opposition, where 'funders often view education as a luxury alongside the essential needs of water, food, and shelter' (p. 152), Sinclair reviewed reports of psychosocial trauma in young children, concluding the necessity for early educational responses in order to make emotional and social healing possible, since these factors assist in restoring a sense of normalcy and hope.

Consequently, the Rapid Response Education Program was developed to help children from Freetown, Sierra Leone in the aftermath of the 1999 violence there. Research on this programme indicated evidence of healing measures in just two weeks following its implementation. Sinclair reported that recurrent mental pictures of traumatic events fell by 8 percent, sleep difficulties decreased by 49 percent and more than half of the children interviewed reported feeling relief 'when they drew pictures, wrote, or talked about their war experiences' (Sinclair, 2001, p. 156). Nearly two decades later, a small number of psychologists and counsellors have been attempting to alleviate the psychological distress and trauma of young refugees caught up in the Myanmar/Bangladesh tragedy in similar ways, as reported by Bennett (2017).

Language and literacy learning

The second most common category of needs among children in refugee camps, according to Sinclair (2001, p. 1), was 'language acquisition'. In reality, the issue of language and literacy for many refugee children/students is many-sided and it is important that its complexity is recognised. In the case of Arab refugee children in Jordan, the language issue is comparatively straightforward. Arabic is the language of the people with whom they have sought refuge, and although there are variations in pronunciations and spoken dialects, Arabic is the language they hear in the local community, use in the mosque if they are Muslim and in the school classroom with teachers and other students.

In Lebanon, Arab refugee children have the advantage of already knowing the language of the local community and the mosque and, in this way, maintaining the language of their home and family in the public sphere. They are confronted, however, with learning a new language for school since Lebanese schools use either English or French as the language of instruction. In order to learn in Lebanese classrooms, they must be able not only to understand and speak, but also to read and write the language of the school. These are fundamental skills that are almost impossible for refugee students to learn from simply being placed in a regular classroom, with teachers following the usual curriculum, as Australian schools discovered in the 1950s and 1960s, when they were dealing with post-World War II refugees from Europe (Smolicz, 1999).

Those refugee children who are accepted for settlement in Australia or Sweden face a different language challenge. Both for communicating in the local community and for learning at school, they must learn to understand and speak, as well as read and write, a new language – English in Australia and Swedish in Sweden. Over time, exposure to the new language at school in everyday life and in the media becomes overwhelming. The times and places where they can use Arabic is severely restricted to home, Syrian refugee friends and the mosque (Maadad, 2018). The emotional comfort and sense of security that comes to human beings from being able to speak their home language openly and freely is denied them.

Learning the language of the host country and its education system quickly and effectively gives refugee students considerable benefits for their future lives. Equally important, maintaining and developing their home language are among the best ways of overcoming the psychological trauma of their refugee experience through the sense of familiarity and control they feel when they are able to express themselves in a language they know. It also provides them with positive affirmation of their cultural identity, as well as a sense of their acceptance and worth in the new country. The psychologists working in the Bangladesh camp recognised this when they set up their programme for Rohingya refugee children to learn in their home language.

Responding to refugee students' future-oriented needs

Once refugee students have reached their country of settlement, there are ongoing and new concerns to be met. The basic needs for successful adjustment remain those outlined by Sinclair (2001) for refugee children in emergency situations in camps. The challenge is for schools and teachers to meet the needs of 'stressed and traumatized children' through programmes that reinforce their sense of being safe, strengthen their sense of self, provide the opportunity to learn about the host country and its culture, while maintaining their connections as far as possible to their own home and family culture. Successful adaptation to schooling in the host country, gaining mastery in the language of the host country and maintaining, or even gaining, literacy in their home language all take on a new importance.

Dealing with continuing trauma

Many educational practitioners and researchers have taken up the pedagogical challenge of teaching refugee students who continue to exhibit trauma and anxieties in regular school classrooms by using approaches based on Freire's critical theory and Boal's *Theatre of the Oppressed*. One such scholar was Schroeter (2013, p. 395), who in a study based on critical pedagogy explored 'notions of identity, belonging, and culture with francophone secondary students' in Canadian schools. She described 'the process whereby Black African-Canadian students with refugee backgrounds identified their program, as well as their language, citizenship status, and race as factors limiting their imagined social futures' (p. 395).

Schroeter's work showed how creative learning spaces and opportunities enabled students to tell their teachers, administrators, and educational researchers about their feelings and experiences. She recognised, however, that encouraging refugee students to talk 'about the problems they face in school entails taking the risk that we may be told things we do not want to hear' (p. 396). Schroeter asked the question: 'Who wants to learn that their efforts to meet students' needs have accentuated feelings of marginalization?' (p. 395). Following on from Freire's (1996) idea that 'in order for education to become liberating, students must be involved in examining oppressive social realities', Schroeter provided a venue for students to identify the problems they face in school, while at the same time recognising that these might not be liberating for all students (Schroeter, 2013, p. 396).

One of the approaches used was based directly on Boal's *Theatre of the Oppressed* method. How it worked in practice is described below in detail (Norbrega et al., 2017, p. 19):

> Every situation is first played continuously in a way that leads to a disaster or at least an unsatisfactory resolution of the depicted conflict (in terms of classical drama composition it stands for exposition and collision). In the second step, the situation is acted out again from the beginning, but spectator now becomes a spect-actor, who can at any time stop the play, substitute any of the actors on the scene and start with different behaviour which then inevitably influences the development of the situation. Any spectator can stop the play at any time and substitute the previous actor in the role, therefore the boundary between actors and viewers is erased ... As this is not only theatre

but also an educational method, it is very desirable to incorporate a reflection phase when all the spect-actors summarize the course of events, with a special focus on the game-changing events, unwind their emotions and generalize the principles learned.

In line with earlier Australian research (see Luke, 1997), Schroeter (2013, p. 396) argued that providing such classroom theatre-based teaching/learning experiences enabled 'educators to learn about the ways students interpret their experiences'. She warned, however, that such pedagogies, were 'not a straightforward process; innovative pedagogies are needed to garner student interest, as are research methodologies that can capture complex, fluid, and dynamic school contexts and identities' (p. 396). In discussing her results, she argued that 'students' discussions and performances showed how programmatic placement can amplify feelings of exclusion in a society where language and race form the basis upon which one's citizenship can be called into question' (p. 396).

Earlier research had revealed the powerful extent of classroom-based theatre/drama pedagogies (e.g. Gallagher and Lortie, 2007), and Schroeter's (2013) case study generated insights 'into the way critical ... pedagogies can create spaces for marginalized students to explore the problems they experience in school'. Indeed, for Schroeter (2013, p. 398) 'this is significant because allowing students to express themselves and test out their theories about life is important if they are to feel valued and empowered'. Fundamental to this is the adoption of a critical literacy approach that recognises the multiple literacies of many students from refugee backgrounds, and makes use of life histories for cultural learning and the learning of new information. Such recognition of the realities of their situation is an important way for teachers to reach out to refugee children (Quintero, 2009). Students from refugee backgrounds benefit from an emphasis on what they know and value; it will – through transformative education and resilience building – encourage their emancipation from dehumanising situations (Maadad and Rodwell, 2017).

School educational policy and traumatised refugee children

The best-selling author, David Bornstein, asked the following question: 'What good are the best teachers or schools if the most vulnerable kids feel so unsafe that they are unavailable to learn?' (2013a). Earlier, Bornstein (2013b) had commented on 'the damaging effects that prolonged stress can have on young children who lack adequate protection from adults'. He explained how over the past 15 years, researchers such as Lyons-Ruth et al. (2003) had found that highly stressful – and potentially traumatic – childhood experiences are more prevalent than previously understood (Bornstein, 2013a); now scientists were developing good insights on the mechanisms through which they change the brain and body. Bornstein illustrated a variety of scenarios where legislation has been implemented or was being reviewed for its success in facilitating students' mental health. He concluded:

Making sure that schools and other social services are sensitized in these ways is not just about assisting those children who have endured extreme stress. It's not just about helping them get through school, either. It's about taking care of everyone. Just as we send a powerful message about our values when we make accommodations for people with disabilities, schools send powerful messages by the way they treat children whose behaviour falls outside the normal bounds. They can mete out punishment in ways that reinforce judgments and hierarchies and perpetuate crises – or respond by deepening the understanding about others and building supportive communities. This isn't soft-headed thinking; it's the only approach that makes any sense.

Now, these insights have begun to impact on education policies in a multitude of ways, not least the schooling of refugee children, and even the provisions made for those in overseas refugee camps.

Mental health provisions for refugee children in Australian settings

Principals and teachers in countries hosting these young refugees have looked for ways to recognise and also overcome the manifest trauma they revealed in the school environment. Such children were susceptible to repeated thoughts about experiences of violence, feeling afraid and sad, experiencing symptoms of ill health, having difficulty in sleeping, feeling restless and lacking in self-confidence. The publication, *A Teacher's Guide to Working with Students from Refugee and Displaced Backgrounds* produced by the Queensland Program of Assistance to Survivors of Torture and Trauma, sets out support strategies to help refugee children, specifically designed to enable them to better integrate into normal school and classroom activities. Their recommendations included (2007, pp. 4, 8):

- providing refugee students with appropriate responsibilities to improve self-confidence and reduce disciplinary issues;
- providing avenues for them to develop close relationships with other students;
- teaching the students about Australia and Australian culture;
- consolidating links with refugee children's families;
- linking students and their families to additional support systems; and
- encouraging opportunities for children to talk about their culture and some of their experiences.

Clearly, from initial placement in intermediary refugee camps in countries such as Bangladesh or Lebanon to schools in those countries which offer permanent settlement, such as Australia and Sweden, mental health is an important issue that needs to be resolved with appropriate provisions.

Appropriate school structures

Importantly for educational authorities, although Schroeter's research (2013) emphasised the need for developing pedagogies based on students' needs, age and academic ability, she did not consider that these factors should necessarily be the criteria by which classes were organised:

> Further research is needed to identify other educational alternatives for addressing the needs of youths with refugee backgrounds. Perhaps these might include making instructional adaptations in mainstream classes so that streaming is avoided and these students are not placed in separate programs that may heighten feelings of exclusion and marginalization.

Such adaptations to school organisation and structure for refugees students have been advocated in a recent United Nations Educational Scientific and Cultural Organisation report and by a number of other writers as well. In schools with significant numbers of refugee students, who perhaps demonstrated heightened levels of anxiety and dispositions towards mental disorders, it has been argued that there is a clear need for educational policy makers and administrators to consider increased inclusion in the local schools of host countries rather than segregation, access to psychosocial support, less conventional groupings of students such as vertical groupings and ability-based, language-support programmes (UNESCO, 2018; Morrison, 2013; Dupriez, 2010). These are some of the macro-level adaptations that can be carried out by education policy makers and administrators. On a micro level, adaptations can be easier to achieve and particularly relevant in school or outside organised extra-curricular activities, such as scouting, music and other clubs. Applying the principles of the *Theatre of the Oppressed* (Boal, 1985), in the form of a pedagogy of the oppressed and a pedagogy of the displaced, may also be adapted to the explicit teaching of subjects wherever appropriate.

Settlement and schooling policies

Once settled in the host country, there is a more urgent emphasis on learning related directly to the immediate host context and their future within it. It is at this point that the host country's settlement policy for immigrants, and refugee students' schooling in particular, has to be taken into account as the newcomers consider their future possibilities. Taking the example of the United States, settlement and schooling policies have been based on assimilation, the general expectation that new arrivals would eventually merge into the mainstream groups of society and become more or less indistinguishable from those Americans who arrived some generations earlier. According to Zhou (1997, p. 976), assimilation was based on the assumptions that there is a natural process by which diverse ethnic groups come to share a common culture and gain equal access to the opportunity structure of society; that the process consists of gradually deserting old cultures and behavioural patterns in favour of new ones; and that, once set in motion, this process moves inevitably and irreversibly towards assimilation.

Over the last few decades, there has been growing recognition that assimilation needed to be understood in more specific ways, in terms of new arrivals assimilating to particular groups in society, since in fact many immigrant groups have been able to maintain their own community life outside the mainstream. Moreover, the fact that refugee students arrived with quite different levels of educational achievement has been acknowledged. As a result the idea of 'segmented assimilation' as a practical policy for schools has been developed (Portes and Zhou, 1993; Zhou, 1997). It was intended to take account of the different trauma experiences, diverse entry situations and varying levels of previous schooling when refugee students were accepted into a particular school situation. The implementation of this policy meant assessing each child's point of need at the time of entry. Often the most important initial factor was the level of manifested trauma.

The strategy of assimilation has long been taken for granted in Sweden, which has a policy of accepting single young refugees, a group that most other countries have been reluctant to accept. For Sweden, the concept of integration was introduced into politics and policies during the 1970s as part of the debate on multiculturalism (Borevi, 2013). By the 1990s, Sweden was celebrated, alongside Australia and Canada, as a successful example of immigrant integration into the host society. Wiesbrock (2011) more recently contended that even in the wake of the 9/11 attacks, integration/assimilation policies in Sweden continued to be generally effective and avoided what has been termed 'more coercive forms of civic integration' (p. 18). Despite the fact that national security did become a priority and some European countries, such as the United Kingdom and the Netherlands, began to retreat from the policy aims of multiculturalism, Sweden continued to be depicted as a nation unaffected by this evolving 'multiculturalism crisis' and as a clear example of 'positive' immigrant multiculturalism in Europe (Borevi, 2013, p. 140).

Yet within Sweden itself the debate has become more critical and the definition of integration or assimilation continues to be fought. With no resources of their own, no family members and no community of earlier arrivals within Sweden, the only chance for these young refugees to survive and make good was to make the most of the opportunities offered at school and learn the Swedish language and ways of life as quickly as possible. It was recognised, however, that this would be a gradual process that could take years to achieve. In the meantime, to support the adjustment to what was a new and alien way of life to them, they were given the opportunity to continue the study of their mother tongue as an option in the primary school curriculum (South Australian Institute of Languages, 1995).

Australia's experience of accepting refugees goes back to the displaced persons in refugee camps in Central Europe after World War II. The assumption was that these people and their children would assimilate into mainstream Australian society. By the late 1960s and early 1970s it was becoming quite clear that assimilation was not happening in many cases. Refugee and immigrant groups had developed their own community life which was attractive to many families and this pattern was found in first- and second-generation 'new arrivals' to Australia. The parents of children born in Australia were anxious that their offspring should learn the language of the home. By the mid-1970s, a new multicultural policy was accepted by both major political parties federally and on a state level in the legislation passed by the South Australian, New South Wales and Victorian parliaments. In the Australian context, 'multiculturalism recognises and affirms the diverse cultural, ethnic and linguistic backgrounds of Australian people and provides equality of opportunity and outcomes for all Australians regardless of their backgrounds' (Matwijiw, 1988).

For the next 20 years both Liberal and Labor governments maintained and developed this policy in various ways and provided the funds needed for its implementation. Furthermore, these governments were open and compassionate to the plight of refugees, accepting in particular boat people from Vietnam, families from Cambodia and later women and children from South Sudan. From the late 1990s and early 2000s this openness was replaced by a hard-line emphasis on border protection to keep out illegal boat people (Hasmath and McKenzie, 2013). However, in some states the multicultural recognition and acceptance of bilingual and bicultural diversity as a worthwhile value for the whole of Australian society continues to have important implications for language learning in schools, particularly for refugee students.

Language and literacy needs for the future

Language learning becomes the central focus of initial education in the country of settlement. Where these programmes are successful, they can provide the most effective means of overcoming the trauma and stress of the past through offering hope in possibilities for the future. The importance and complexities of developing a good languages education policy in a plural society such as Australia are considered in a detailed discussion of 'language as a bridge or a barrier' (Smolicz, 1999). On arrival in South Australia, for example, refugee students have had access to at least six months of immersion classes in English as an additional language and for most refugee groups, the opportunity to continue learning their own home language. Indeed, in the case of both the Cambodian and South Sudanese refugee students in South Australia, the disruptions caused by civil wars in their home countries meant that many had their first opportunity to gain literacy in their home language (Khymer and Dinka, respectively) here in their country of settlement. From another perspective, having available bilingual teachers and school aides who can speak with students in their home language has proved most helpful in dealing with students' trauma.

Being able to communicate in their home language or mother tongue represents a deep-seated psychological, social and cultural need of human beings. Furthermore, the intellectual, aesthetic, artistic and literary benefits of gaining full literacy in it are considerable. These benefits have led almost every new group of refugees arriving in South Australia since the late 1970s to successfully develop the study of their language as a Year 12 subject that counts for university entrance. In the states of Victoria, South Australia and New South Wales, the principle exists of recognising a refugee or immigrant's group language as a Year 12 subject, for instance Vietnamese, Khymer, Dinka and Persian. Arabic, established earlier in New South Wales and Victoria, became available in South Australia in 2000. The availability of these subjects has contributed in an important practical way to those students wanting to go on to university studies since they were often able to gain quite high scores in their home language subject. This became evident in a research study on Cambodian students who were undertaking university studies in Adelaide (Smolicz et al., 2003). Another study of Dinka-speaking South Sudanese refugee students attending South Australian secondary schools revealed that they were intending to follow a similar path in their efforts to gain university entrance (Thomas, 2017).

Another important dimension in language learning in Australia has been the role played by independent schools. Australia's long-standing commitment to religious freedom, written into the constitution at the time of federation, has allowed the establishment of independent schools based on a particular religious tradition. Linked to this has been the opportunity to include the study of a language other than English which was important to their religious history. The Roman Catholic Church, for example, provides schools for about 30 percent of the school population; some of these were among the first to introduce the teaching of Italian. There is also a smaller network of Lutheran schools, many of whom teach German. There are a few Jewish schools that teach Hebrew and several states have Greek Orthodox schools which teach Modern Greek. All of these are able to provide their languages at Year 12 level as subjects that count for university entrance. These independent religious schools have provided a model for Islamic groups seeking to establish schools for their communities in Australia. Following existing government regulations, they have been able to establish independent schools, run by their own board of governors, teaching the Koran as their religious base and Arabic as a language subject, which can be taken up to Year 12 level.

Countering moral panic-inspired Islamophobia

An emerging challenge to a host country's acceptance of Syrian refugee students and their families has been the nascent issue of moral panic occurring in some Western countries, based on politically and socio-culturally inspired Islamophobia (Barker, 2016). As well as the toxic trauma suffered as part of the civil war between Islamic groups in Syria, young people who are refugees from the Middle East, as well as other predominantly Muslim countries, are finding themselves in a different kind of toxic environment in their host country, in the form of what has been termed 'Islamophobia'. Islamophobia has been defined as:

> the fear or hostility towards followers of [the] Islamic religion. This unjustified fear has contributed immensely to discrimination of Muslims across the globe. It is a base point for seclusion of Muslims in the political arena and affiliate social classes in the society. The phenomenon is characterized by a distinct preassumption of crime or guilt through association. Hate crimes are also a common characteristic of this condition ... The tragic occurrence of September 11th [2001] contributed intensely to the viewing of Islamic religion with suspicion. It fuelled a slew of prejudice, suspicions, hate crimes, as well as fear [of] the Muslims.
>
> *(Alshammari, 2013, p. 177)*

In some Western countries, right-wing political parties have been active through elected members' or party leaders' speeches in parliament and in the organisation of protest rallies, against the presence in their country of Islamic immigrants who were seen as a threat to peace and security in the community. In Australia, for example, the One Nation Party, with the Queensland senator Pauline Hanson as their leader, is very opposed to Muslim immigration generally on the (very debatable) grounds that Muslims do not want to integrate into the wider community. One of her main policies is her demand for a royal commission to determine whether the existence of Islamic groups in Australia poses a security threat to the nation. The party advocates bans not only on all Muslim immigration, but also face-covering veils, the construction of new mosques and halal certification. It also insists on the installation of surveillance cameras in all mosques and Islamic schools (Iner, 2017, p. 17). While this sort of moral panic is being orchestrated by Hanson's cohort, evidence from a study by Forrest et al. (2017), on the population and distribution of immigrants to Australia using data from the 2011 census, showed that Hanson's claim was unfounded.

By 2017, Islamophobia in Australia had reached new levels with Muslim women being prime victims. For instance, a study showed that close to 80 percent of Muslim women with head coverings reported being abused physically, verbally and online (Hegarty, 2017). Other anecdotal reports of Islamophobia included anonymous death threat letters being dropped in mailboxes, while Muslim children walking home from school were being shouted at and had toy guns pointed at them (Siddique, 2017). *Inter alia*, a national report, entitled *Islamophobia in Australia* showed how schools and school surroundings were often settings for the expression of this phobia (Iner, 2017, p. 4). A few months after the release of the above-mentioned report, the One Nation Party staged a provocative stunt that invited worldwide controversy and represented a bizarre attempt at gaining publicity. National television news showed Pauline Hanson appearing in the Australian Senate in a burqa. Following this Hanson spectacle, horrified Australians awoke to the news of an ISIS-inspired massacre in Barcelona, Spain (ABC News, 2017), as if providing proof to some people of the Islamic risk. This is one example of the way Islamophobia has negatively impacted on Australian society.

Since the 9/11 terrorist attacks on New York in September 2001 and the massive increase in global migration patterns as a consequence of the Middle East crisis, most Western countries have been affected by Islamophobia in some way. This has resulted in 'moral panic' focused on aspects of racism and Islamophobia. Brenda Cohen and Muhamad-Bradner (2012), in their systematic analysis of the phenomenon of moral panic, demonstrated that many people in the wider society were engaging in behaviour associated with a moral panic as a result of recently arrived migrant communities, especially Islamic ones, being represented by the media as 'folk devils'. It seems obvious that most of these sorts of attitudes have emerged since the events of 9/11. In cases such as these the mainstream media and increasingly the social media were immediately fed into the daily news cycles in the United States, the United Kingdom and Australia. The glaring fact is that although we do not understand fully the impact of such politically, culturally and socially prompted influences such as Islamophobia, the role played by such media-inspired moral panic can have a direct effect on young people in schools. Subsequently, their opportunities to achieve effectively in their host society, particularly through good schooling, can be greatly compromised. It should also be recognised that such hostility towards Syrian refugees stands in sharp contrast to the prevailing attitudes in Australian society from the 1970s to the 1990s toward earlier waves of refugees, such as the Vietnamese boat people, Khymer and Dinka families (Smolicz et al., 2003; Thomas, 2017).

Conclusion

With devastating social crises occurring in countries such as Myanmar and Syria during the second decade of the twenty-first century, children are clearly the most affected victims. From an international perspective, the obvious nature of distress appears to be closely linked to issues of mental health. In hastily constructed schools in refugee camps, often in neighbouring countries such as Lebanon (to Syria) and Bangladesh (to Myanmar), international aid organisations call for the assistance of social workers and psychologists such as those reported by Bennett (2017). School buildings, teachers and having a curriculum are important, but for the many students suffering from mental health issues, and many of them severe, little learning is possible until their mental health is first attended to.

For those young people who have relocated in a foreign country, these mental health matters pose important challenges to theories of segmented assimilation. Now, teachers, psychologists and educational bureaucrats are increasingly recognising the importance of the word 'segmented' in the term, because each individual will approach the assimilation process from their own point of need. Significantly, theorists are recognising that segmented assimilation is continually evolving in order to embrace new demands. This is recognised by governments and education authorities such as those in Queensland. Other challenges are thrown out for refugee students, and segmented assimilation theory in the form of Islamophobia-inspired moral panic, often at the bidding of politicians. Finally, in the classrooms of these host-country schools, teachers and theorists are recognising the potential and powerful role of classroom-based critical and theatre/drama pedagogies in improving refugee students' mental health from the outset and their overall life and well-being in general.

References

ABC News (2017). '7yo Australian Boy Missing after Barcelona Attack, Mum in Hospital'. Retrieved 18 August 2017 from www.abc.net.au/news/.

Albert, Eleanor (2018). 'The Rohingya Crisis'. Council on Foreign Relations. Retrieved 23 August 2018 from www.cfr.org/backgrounder/rohingya-crisis.

Alshammari, Dalal (2013). 'Islamophobia'. *International Journal of Humanities and Social Science*, vol. 3, no. 15, pp. 177–180.

Barker, I. (2016). 'Teachers Warn Nicky Morgan of Racism in Schools Following Brexit Vote'. *TES*, 1 July. Retrieved 11 November 2017 from www.tes.com/news/school-news/breaking-news/teachers-warn-nicky-morgan-racism-schools-following-brexit-vote.

Barmania, Sima (2011). 'Why Paulo Freire's "Pedagogy of the Oppressed" Is Just as Relevant Today as Ever'. Saybrook University. Retrieved 23 August 2018 from www.saybrook.edu/blog/2011/11/18/why-paulo-freireaos-aoipedagogy-oppressedao%C2%9D-just-relevant-today-ever/.

Bennett, J. (2017). 'Rohingya Refugees Suffer Unspeakable Acts of Cruelty at the Hands of Myanmar's Military'. *ABC News*, 11 November. Retrieved 20 November 2017 from www.abc.net.au/news/2017-11-11/traumatised-rohingya-refugees-tell-harrowing-tales/9140912.

Boal, A. (1985 [1979]). *Theatre of the Oppressed*, trans. C.A. Leal McBride and M. Leal McBride. New York: Theatre Communications Group.

Borevi, K. (2013). 'Understanding Swedish Multiculturalism'. In P. Kivisto and O. Wahlbeck (eds), *Debating Multiculturalism in the Nordic Welfare States* (pp. 140–169). Basingstoke: Palgrave Macmillan.

Bornstein, D. (2013a). 'Schools that Separate the Child from the Trauma'. *New York Times*, 13 November. Retrieved 23 November 2017 from https://opinionator.blogs.nytimes.com/2013/11/13/separating-the-child-from-the-trauma/.

Bornstein, D. (2013b). 'Protecting Children from Toxic Stress'. *New York Times*, 30 October. Retrieved 29 November 2017 from https://opinionator.blogs.nytimes.com/2013/10/30/protecting-children-from-toxic-stress/.

Brown, G. (2016). 'Without Education, Syria's Children Will Be a Lost Generation'. *Guardian*, 13 January. Retrieved 20 November 2017 from www.theguardian.com/commentisfree/2016/jan/12/syria-refugee-children-lebanon-double-shift-schools.

Calamur, Krishnadev (2017). 'The Misunderstood Roots of Burma's Rohingya Crisis'. *Atlantic*. Retrieved 23 August 2018 from www.theatlantic.com/international/archive/2017/09/rohingyas-burma/540513/.

Cherri, Rima and Hariri, Houssam (2018). 'Lebanon Puts in an Extra Shift to Get Syrian Refugees into School'. *UNHCR: The UN Refugee Agency*, 26 June. Retrieved 5 March

2019 from www.unhcr.org/news/stories/2018/6/5b321c864/lebanon-puts-extra-shift-syrian-refugees-school.html.

Children on the Edge (2018). 'Education for Rohingya Refugee Children'. Retrieved 27 August 2018 from www.childrenontheedge.org/bangladesh-education-for-rohingya-refugee-children.html.

Cohen, B. and Muhamad-Bradner, C. (2012). 'A School for Scandal: Rütli High School and German Press'. In G. Morgan and S. Poynting (eds), *Global Islamophobia: Muslims and Moral Panic in the West*. Farnham: Ashgate.

Culbertson, S., Ling, T., Henham, M.-L., Corbett, J., Karam, R., Pankowska, P., Saunders, C., Bellasio, J. and Baruch, B. (2016). *Evaluation of the Emergency Education Response for Syrian Refugee Children and Host Communities in Jordan*. Santa Monica, CA: RAND Corporation. Retrieved 5 March 2019 from www.rand.org/pubs/research_reports/RR1203.html.

Dupriez, D. (2010). *Methods of Grouping Learners at School*. Paris: United Nations Educational, Scientific and Cultural Organization.

Forrest, J., Johnston, R., Siciliano, F., Manley, D. and Jones, K. (2017). Are Australia's Suburbs Swamped by Asians and Muslims? Countering Political Claims with Data. *Australian Geographer*, 48(4), 457–472. doi: doi:10.1080/00049182.2017.1329383.

Freire, P. (1995). *Pedagogy of Hope: Reliving Pedagogy of the Oppressed*. New York: Continuum International Publishing Group.

Freire, P. (1997 [1968]). *Pedagogy of the Oppressed*, trans. M. Ramos. London: Penguin Education.

Gallagher, K. and Lortie, P. (2007). 'Building Theories of Their Lives: Youth Engaged in Drama Research'. In D. Thiessen and A. Cook-Sather (eds), *International Handbook of Student Experience in Elementary and Secondary School* (pp. 405–437). Dordrecht: Springer.

Guba, E. G. and Lincoln, Y. S. (1994). 'Competing Paradigms in Qualitative Research'. In N. K. Denzin and Y. S. Lincoln (eds), *Handbook of Qualitative Research* (pp. 105–117). London: Sage.

Hasmath, R. and McKenzie, J. (2013). 'Deterring the 'Boat People': Explaining the Australian Government's People Swap Response to Asylum Seekers'. *Australian Journal of Political Science*, 48(4), 417–430.

Hegarty, S. (2017). Islamophobia: Women Wearing Head Coverings Most at Risk of Attacks, Study Finds. Retrieved 12 July 2018, from www.abc.net.au/news/2017-07-10/hijab-wearing-women-most-at-risk-of-islamophobic-attacks/8688856.

Iner, D. (ed.) (2017). 'Islamophobia in Australia'. Retrieved 19 August 2017 from https://arts-ed.csu.edu.au/__data/assets/pdf_file/0009/2811960/csu-islamophobia-in-australia-July-update-digital-after-launch.pdf.

Luke, A. (1997). 'Genres of Power: Literacy Education and the Production of Capital'. In R. Hasan and G. Williams (eds), *Literacy in Society* (pp. 308–338). London: Longman.

Lyons-Ruth, K., Yellin, C., Melnick, S. and Atwood, G. (2003). 'Childhood Experiences of Trauma and Loss Have Different Relations to Maternal Unresolved and Hostile-Helpless States of Mind on the AAI'. *Attachment and Human Development*, 5(4), 330–414.

Maadad, N. (2018). *Interviews in Schools in Australia and Sweden*. Unpublished manuscript.

Maadad, N. and Rodwell, G. (2017). *Schooling and Education in Lebanon: Syrian and Syrian Palestinian Refugees inside and outside the Camps*. Bern: Peter Lang.

Mandala Centre for Change (n.d.). *Theatre of the Oppressed*. Retrieved 23 August 2018 from www.mandalaforchange.com/site/applied-theatre/theatre-of-the-oppressed/.

Matwijiw, P. (1988). 'Public Policy on Immigration'. In James Jupp (ed.), *The Australian People: An Encyclopedia of the Nation, Its People and Their Origins*. Sydney: Angus and Robertson.

Morrison, N. (2013). 'Vertical Teaching Returns: Could It Work for Your School?' *Guardian*, 8 January. Retrieved 27 November 2017 from www.theguardian.com/teacher-network/2013/jan/07/vertical-teaching-early-exam-entry.

Norbrega, Lourenço et al. (eds) (2017). *Working with Migrants and Refugees: Guidelines, Tools and Methods*. Prague: International Young Naturefriends.

Panella, Amanda (2016). 'Refugees in Lebanon Benefit from Double-Shift Schools'. *Borgen Project*, 23 July. Retrieved 5 March 2019 from https://borgenproject.org/refugees-in-lebanon-benefit-from-double-shift-schools/.

Portes, A. and Zhou, M. (1993). 'The New Second Generation: Segmented Assimilation and Its Variants', *Annals of the American Academy of Political and Social Science*, 530, 74–96.

Queensland Program of Assistance to Survivors of Torture & Trauma (2007). *A Teacher's Guide to Working with Students from Refugee and Displaced Backgrounds*. Retrieved 23 November 2017 from http://qpastt.org.au/tbcwp1/wp-content/uploads/2014/05/School-teachers-guide-2007-updated-2104.pdf.

Quintero, E. (2009). *Refugee and Immigrant Family Voices*. Rotterdam: Sense Publishers.

Save the Children (2018). *Fight for the Future: Annual Report 2017*. Retrieved 31 August 2018 from www.savethechildren.org.uk/content/dam/global/reports/1280_StC_Annual_Report_Front_v21_WEB3.pdf.

Schroeter, S. (2013). '"The Way It Works" Doesn't: Theatre of the Oppressed as Critical Pedagogy and Counternarrative'. *Canadian Journal of Education*, 36(4), 395–415.

Scotland, J. (2012). 'Exploring the Philosophical Underpinnings of Research: Relating Ontology and Epistemology to the Methodology and Methods of the Scientific, Interpretive, and Critical Research Paradigms'. *English Language Teaching*, 5(9), 9–16. doi: doi:10.5539/elt.v5n9p9.

Siddique, R. (2017). 'We Have to Stop Normalising Relentless Islamophobia in Australia'. Retrieved 20 June 2018, from www.theguardian.com/commentisfree/2017/oct/14/we-have-to-stop-normalising-relentless-islamophobia-in-australia.

Sinclair, M. (2001). 'Education in Emergencies'. In J. Crisp, C. Talbot and D.B. Cipollone (eds), *Learning for a Future: Refugee Education in Developing Countries* (pp. 1–84). Lausanne: United Nations Publications.

Sirin, S.R. and Rogers-Sirin, L. (2015). *The Educational and Mental Health Needs of Syrian Refugee Children*. Washington, DC: Migration Policy Institute.

Smitheram, Esther (2017). *Standing in the Gap for Rohingya Refugee Children: A Community Approach to Making Education Possible*. Promising Practices in Refugee Education. Children on the Edge Publications.

Smolicz, J.J. (1999). *Education and Culture*, ed. M. Secombe and J. Zajda. Melbourne: James Nicholas Publishers.

Smolicz, J.J., Yiv, C. and Secombe, M.J. (2003). 'Languages Education as an Empowering Experience: Cambodia Refugees in Multicultural Australia'. In Rolana Terborg (ed.), *Languages and Inequalities*. Mexico, DF: Universidad Nacional Autonoma de Mexico.

South Australian Institute of Languages (1995). Rubichi, R. (eds.) *Why Not Australia? A Cross-National Study of Languages Education Systems*. Adelaide: South Australian Institute of Languages.

Theirworld (2017). 'Rohingya Refugee Children Need Urgent Help to Deal with Their Trauma'. *Reliefweb*, 26 September. Retrieved 25 November 2017 from https://reliefweb.int/report/bangladesh/rohingya-refugee-children-need-urgent-help-deal-their-trauma.

Thomas, J.S. (2017). *From Southern Sudan to Adelaide: Learning Journeys of Refugee Secondary Students*. PhD thesis, School of Education, University of Adelaide.

UNESCO (2018). *Global Education Monitoring Report, 2019: Migration, Displacement and Education: Building Bridges, Not Walls.* Paris: UNESCO.

UNHCR (2019). *Desperate Journeys: January–December 2018.* UN Refugee Agency. Retrieved 5 March 2019 from https://data2.unhcr.org/en/documents/download/67712#_ga=2.80357783.162556866.1551740771-615310502.1551740771.

Walbridge, L.S. and Aziz, T.M. (2000). 'Iraqi Refugees in Detroit'. In N. Abraham and A. Shryock (eds), *Arab Detroit: From Margin to Mainstream.* Detroit, MI: Wayne State University Press.

Wiesbrock, A. (2011). 'The Integration of Immigrants in Sweden: A Model for the European Union?' *International Migration*, 49(4), 48–66.

Williams, Holly (2015). 'EU Searches for Ways to Stem Tide of Migrant "Death Voyages"'. *CBS News*, 20 April. Retrieved 5 March 2019 from www.cbsnews.com/news/eu-searches-for-ways-to-stem-tide-of-migrant-death-voyages/.

Zhou, M. (1997). 'Segmented Assimilation: Issues, Controversies, and Recent Research on the New Second Generation'. *International Migration Review*, 31(4), Special Issue: Immigrant Adaptation and Native-Born Responses in the Making of Americans (Winter), 975–1008.

3
METHODOLOGY

Introduction

The qualitative case study methodology used in this book supports the critical paradigm informed by firstly, the first pedagogy of the oppressed (Freire, 1996 [1968]), which incorporates a pedagogy of hope and peace; and secondly, the practices of the theatre of the oppressed (Boal, 1985 [1979]), otherwise known as the pedagogy of the displaced (see Appendix) (Maadad and Rodwell, 2017). In this chapter the methodological approach to investigating the educational experiences of Syrian refugee children in Australia and Sweden is described. The case study research design of this book is ideal for understanding the schooling experiences of Syrian refugee children and how they try to make sense of their new environments. It follows the format developed by Merriam (1998), Mertens (1998), Stake (2010) and Yin (2009). While this study draws upon a contemporary historical event, the Syrian Refugee Crisis of 2011, the case study research design follows a sociological approach to understanding Syrian refugee children's educational experiences. As LeCompte and Preissle (1993) explain:

> Educational case studies drawing upon sociology have explored such topics as student–peer interactions as a function of high school social structure, the effect of role sets on teachers' interactions with students, the actual versus the hidden school curriculum, the relationship of schooling to equalities and inequalities in society at large, and so on.
>
> *(Cited in Merriam, 1998, p. 37)*

The research process for this book is explained in more detail in the sections below. The methods used were a combination of observation with interviewing, which is an approach that fosters conversation and reflection. This reflective approach encouraged the researcher and study participants to question the 'natural' state of affairs in the particular education system, and the society of which it is a part, and challenge the mechanisms for order maintenance taken for granted in that context.

The data collected in this qualitative research aimed to be rich in the description of people, places and conversations, something that is not easily achieved through statistical procedures. The 'rich description' evolved out of the interview-questionnaire-observation method employed here. It is typical of much qualitative research in that it is concerned with understanding behaviour and events from a subject's own frame of reference. Qualitative researchers believe that the interview-questionnaire-observation method is a very suitable way to document and explain experiences (Guion et al., 2011). It is in fact the meaning of our experiences that constitutes our reality. The data were collected through sustained contact with people in the settings where they normally spend their time. Participants' observations and in-depth interviewing are the two most common ways to collect data. The researcher in this case enters the world of the people being studied, gets to know, be known and trusted by them, and systematically keeps a detailed written record of what is uttered and observed. In the course of this book and in the following chapters, the materials are supplemented by many other data in the form of relevant policy documents especially from Australia and Sweden, research findings of people and global and local organisations who deal with refugee matters, media reports, examples of schooling events and insightful and detailed commentaries. Taking such an all-encompassing approach helps to 'overcome gaps and challenges including poor data, inadequate models, insufficient information sharing, inaccessible, non-comparable and fragmented knowledge affecting the community working on migration and demography' (Amran and Urso, 2016, p. 10).

Case study design

This qualitative case study methodology involved the use of multiple sources of data and methods of collection, as it attempted to present and explain the complexity of the situation of Syrian refugee children in their schools in the host country (Yin, 2009; Amran and Urso, 2016, p. 52). The comparative component of the case study design attempted to describe and explain the similarities and differences of the experiences of Syrian refugee children in the two host countries, yet being mindful of not reducing these differences to stereotypes and avoiding overarching generalisations that simplify our understanding of Syrian refugee children's experience (Stake, 2010).

For the purpose of this book, both descriptive and explanatory case study types have been utilised. As a descriptive research method, the researcher purposefully scoped the nature and extent of Syrian refugee children's educational experiences in Australia and Sweden in a way that served as a useful precursor to a more in-depth explanatory analysis, entailing the use of critical paradigms discussed in Chapter 2. The descriptive element of the study, as the name suggests, 'describes' a situation or scenario, subject, behaviour or phenomenon related to the schooling experiences of Syrian refugee children in Australia and Sweden. Descriptive case studies are designed to amass detailed information that can later be used as a basis for comparisons and theoretical explanations or theory building (Merriam, 1998). They provide a rich data set that often brings to light new knowledge or awareness that may have otherwise gone unnoticed or not encountered. It is particularly useful when it is important to gather information without disrupting the activities of participants or when it is not possible to test and measure large numbers of participants. Researchers in this way can observe natural behaviours with nil or minimal effect on the participants' schedules (Creswell, 2013; Harrison et al., 2017). Careful observations and detailed documentation of Syrian refugee children's school experiences have been carried out in this research in two main research sites: Australia and Sweden.

As the explanatory element of this research, data gathered on refugee situations, problems, challenges and schooling behaviours were analysed in the light of the critical paradigms set out in Chapter 2. While descriptive case research examines the what, where and when of the phenomenon, explanatory research seeks answers to why and how types of questions. It attempts to 'connect the dots' in research, by identifying causal factors and outcomes of the target phenomenon (Stake, 2010; Yin, 2009; Merriam, 1998). Examples include understanding the reasons behind responses to the Syrian refugee crisis by the two case study countries, the schooling experience of refugee children and requirements for educational achievement, with the goal of prescribing strategies from critical pedagogy that promote conscientisation (see Nouri and Sajjadi, 2014, pp. 79–80) and emancipation. Seeking explanations for observed and gathered data has required strong theoretical and interpretation skills, along with intuition, insights and personal experience. Critical paradigms have orientated the theoretical and interpretation of data observed and gathered. Additionally, for the purpose of this book, data searches have been generally conducted online using keyword terminology to find the appropriate, most detailed, comprehensive and explanatory primary and secondary sources. A major aim of the process has been to collate all the relevant and most up-to-date, where possible, sources covering demographics, anecdotal and policy-related information and new developments on the ever changing topic of Syrian refugee children's education.

Data-collection methods

As part of a case study design, the main methods employed in collecting information for this study have been observations, surveys and interviews. Observations sought to record and review the actions and behaviours or traits of Syrian refugee children in their natural environment, which, in the case of this book, were conducted in the school environment (Neuman and Neuman, 2006; Rosenthal and

Rosnow, 1991). Additionally, surveys were utilised to gather demographic information and agreement or disagreement to some statements given in the survey. In-depth face-to-face interviews conducted either with individual respondents or with groups have also been useful modes of data collection.

Observation

The observation method was organised with the schools in both countries to spend a few hours per day in several classrooms observing students' behaviour, participation, interaction and communication. A total of six hours per class (over three sessions) were committed to classes teaching a variety of subjects and allowing observation of different pedagogical approaches and teachers. This method worked really well in that it generated interesting information from both countries. Note taking was the main recording process and we were allowed to take photos of information on the board and the classroom settings. Being in class with the participants proved to be an important research experience. In one way, it strengthened the trust between us and the students, and encouraged them to respond so they could impress us. In another way, the students were distracted because they wanted to talk to us in Arabic and ask questions. Our hope was to successfully and accurately translate in order to facilitate their understanding.

Survey

At the first stage of data collection, a set of short questions was emailed to the teachers who had agreed to distribute it to the students participating in the study. The purpose of this was to develop a relationship between the students and the researcher, and prepare them for the later and a longer questionnaire, and the eventual interview to follow. It is worth mentioning that all 100 participants (50 in Australia and 50 in Sweden) responded to their teacher's request and agreed to continue with the subsequent stages of the study. A few weeks later we met face to face in Sweden with all the Swedish participants in order to get to know each other, and they were handed the longer questionnaire to complete prior to our interviews with them a few days later. A similar process was followed in Australia a month later where we met the participants in groups and gave them the questionnaire prior to the interviews. The longer questionnaire proved to be very effective in allowing them to express insightful and more detailed thoughts and feelings about their experiences.

Interview

In order to provide a credible picture of the educational experiences of Syrian refugee children, this book is largely based on interviews with a total of 100 refugee children, who had been selected purposively. Half of these children were interviewed in Sweden and the other half in Australia. Additionally, parents and caregivers/guardians (n = 15), teachers (n = 12), school principals (n = 4), administrators (n = 4) and educational policy makers (n = 2), making up a total of 37 additional participants from both countries who were interviewed. In total, for both Australia and Sweden, 137 individuals participated in the data collection. Appropriate ethical research protocols were met prior to the actual interviews. Information about the study was explained to the participants and informed consent was secured. Anonymity of participants and confidentiality of their responses were assured. Risks associated with harm in the process of data collection, such as participants having to recall traumatic experiences that might cause distress, were dealt with by having school counsellors aware of the interview and observation sessions and on standby in the event that students needed to see them. Additionally, participants were informed that they could withdraw at any time from the interview, the observation or the study itself. The participants were selected through the assistance of gatekeepers of the community, including the education department contact persons for schools in Australia. Social workers and psychologists working with Syrian refugee students in Sweden were contacted through the school principals and teachers involved.

Different interview formats prove useful for case study designs: structured, semi-structured and unstructured. Firstly, the structured interviews consisted of a series of predetermined questions that all interviewees could answer in the same order. This proved to be helpful for the collection of demographic data and Likert-type information. The data analysis tended to be more straightforward because the researcher could compare and contrast different answers given to the same questions. Secondly, unstructured interviews, usually the least reliable, were used to allow for a more informal and conversational mode of data collection, which allowed the participants to direct the interview situation so that the power dynamic between researcher and respondent became fluid and assumed the nature of an egalitarian dialogue between individuals (Kvale, 1996, 2006). Unstructured interviews to some extent can be associated with a high level of respondent bias and comparison of answers given by different respondents tended to be difficult to organise due to the variations in the formulation of questions. Thirdly, the semi-structured interviews used for this research contained components of both structured and unstructured interviews. The author in her capacity as interviewer for this study conducted the semi-structured interviews and prepared a set of the same questions to be answered by all interviewees. At the same time, it was possible to ask additional questions during the interviews so that certain issues, topics or themes could be further clarified.

The main advantage of the interviews included the possibility of collecting detailed information about the educational experience of Syrian refugee children. Moreover, in this type of primary data collection, the researcher can control the process and flow of information and the opportunity to clarify certain issues if and when necessary. On the other hand, the disadvantages included more time required for interviews, together with travel requirements and difficulties associated with arranging an appropriate time and place with the prospective interviewees to conduct interviews. This was certainly experienced in bringing together the data for this book, given the large distances to be covered not only in Australia, but also internationally. The author was mindful of the fact that conducting interviews required an open mind and refraining from any display disagreement in any form when the viewpoints expressed by interviewees contradicted her ideas or assumptions. Moreover, the timing and the place for these interviews had to be effectively scheduled. Specifically, interviews needed to be conducted in a relaxed environment, free of any form of pressure for interviewees whatsoever.

Data analysis

The method of analysis included iterative processes of description of experience, the generation of meanings through categorisation and comparisons, and interpretation of data in terms of themes that connected to critical paradigms. Together the results of these different forms of analysis built up a coherent and theoretically based interpretation of the educational experiences of Syrian refugee children in the two case study countries, Australia and Sweden. Emerging themes and concepts were examined from both micro dimensions (those of the refugee children and their families) and macro dimensions (school, community and country). These themes included rights, education opportunities, learning, teaching, empowerment, freedom/emancipation, socio-economic disadvantage, well-being, culture, language, change/transformation, hope, peace and justice, among others, as well as conscientisation (Freire's term for critical consciousness of one's situation; see Nouri and Sajjadi, 2014, pp. 79–80). While the study did not endeavour to make sweeping generalisations about Syrian refugee children's experiences, it did aim to formulate a more generalised theory (Yin, 2009). Figure 3.1 outlines the iterative process of data analysis used in this book.

Conclusion

The case study methodological design utilised in this book specified two purposes: descriptive and explanatory. Together they helped us understand the development of power structures in education and the areas of enquiry such as language, social relationships, organisational structures, politics, media, cultural ideologies, interpersonal relationships, etc. It is also for the purposes of this book a form of cultural study, which concentrates on understanding the real-life experiences of people, examining communication exchanges within the context of implied power structures and accomplishing positive social change from better education systems as a result. The considerable data collected from observations, surveys and interviews enabled the researcher to present themes for descriptive analyses of the educational experiences of Syrian refugee children in Australia and Sweden. The exploratory

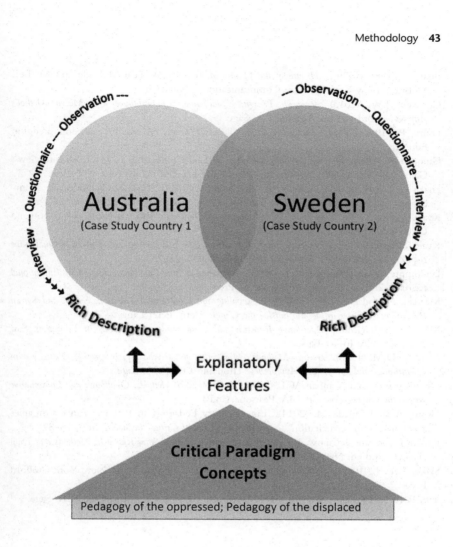

element of the case study design allowed for the generation of meanings for these experiences and utilised the critical framework informed by Freire's pedagogy of the oppressed and related critical paradigms. Thus, analytical generalisations on the educational experiences of Syrian refugee children were able to be generated.

References

Amran, G. and UrsoG. (eds) (2016). 'Gaps and Challenges in the Knowledge of Migration and Demography: Proposals for New Approaches and Solutions'. JRC Science for Policy Report, European Commission. PUBSY No. 104985. Retrieved 28 February 2019 from http://publications.jrc.ec.europa.eu/repository/bitstream/JRC104985/final_report_pubsy_reviewed_1601%281%29.pdf.

Boal, A. (1985 [1979]). *Theatre of the Oppressed*, trans. C.A. Leal McBride and M. Leal McBride. New York: Theatre Communications Group.

Creswell, J.W. (2013). *Research Design: Qualitative, Quantitative, and Mixed Methods Approaches*, 3rd ed. Los Angeles, CA: Sage.

Freire, P. (1996 [1968]). *Pedagogy of the Oppressed*, trans. M. Ramos. London: Penguin Education.

Guion, L.A., Diehl, D.C. and McDonald, D. (2011). 'Conducting an In-Depth Interview'. Gainesville, FL: Family Youth and Community Sciences, University of Florida.

Harrison, H., Birks, M., Franklin, R. and Mills, J. (2017). 'Case Study Research: Foundations and Methodological Orientations'. *Forum: Qualitative Social Research*, 18(1).

Kvale, Steinar (1996). *Interviews: An Introduction to Qualitative Research Interviewing*. Thousand Oaks, CA: Sage.

Kvale, Steinar (2006). 'Dominance through Interviews and Dialogues'. *Journal of Qualitative Inquiry*, 12, 480–500. doi: doi:10.1177/1077800406286235.

LeCompte, M.D. and Preissle, J. (1993). *Ethnography and Qualitative Design in Educational Research*, 2nd ed. New York: Academic Press.

Maadad, N. and Rodwell, G. (2017). *Schooling and Education in Lebanon: Syrian and Syrian Palestinian Refugees inside and outside the Camps*. Bern: Peter Lang.

Merriam, S.B. (1998). *Qualitative Research and Case Study Applications in Education*. San Francisco, CA: Jossey-Bass.

Mertens, D.M. (1998). *Research Methods in Education and Psychology: Integrating Diversity with Quantitative and Qualitative Approaches*. Thousand Oaks, CA: Sage.

Neuman, W.L. and Neuman, W.L. (2006). *Social Research Methods: Qualitative and Quantitative Approaches*, 6th ed. Boston, MA: Pearson/AandB.

Nouri, A. and Sajjadi, M. (2014). 'Emancipatory Pedagogy in Practice: Aims, Principles and Curriculum Orientation'. *International Journal of Critical Pedagogy*, 5(2), 76–87.

Rosenthal, R. and Rosnow, R.L. (1991). *Essentials of Behavioral Research: Methods and Data Analysis*, 2nd ed. New York: McGraw-Hill.

Stake, R.E. (2010). *Qualitative Research: Studying How Things Work*. New York: Guilford Press.

Yin, R.K. (2009). *Case Study Research: Design and Methods*. Thousand Oaks, CA: Sage.

4

POLICIES AND EDUCATION FOR REFUGEES IN AUSTRALIA

Aicha Al Shebli says life in the Syrian city of Aleppo was wonderful before the war. Her family had all the privileges of a modern country – doctors, schools and relative safety. But early one morning in April 2013, Ms Al Shebli said their lives changed in an instant. 'I was in the house, in the kitchen making dough for bread ... It was early in the morning. The kids were outside, playing amongst the sheep. It was a nice warm day but then both sides started shelling, the government side and the [Free Syrian Army] side.' One of Ms Al Shebli's sons, Khaled, was inside, sick in bed. When a rocket hit their house it sent a fireball into his bedroom and he suffered horrific burns to his face. 'I believe something in the rocket was toxic, that's what burned his face off. The rest of his body was covered up and only the face was exposed,' Ms Al Shebli said. Khaled Al Shebli has started school again since his latest operation. The family still does not know which side fired the rocket that maimed their son. After the shelling they fled to a refugee camp in north Lebanon where they spent the next nine months. While there, the family came to the attention of an Australian aid worker, who took their plight to the Australian ambassador who helped facilitate three operations for Khaled in Beirut. In December last year, the Al Sheblis were granted refugee status in Australia and moved to Wollongong, south of Sydney. A few weeks ago, Khaled, now seven, had the first of at least five more operations he will undergo in Australia. The nose reconstruction has helped him breathe easier, and just this week Khaled had his first day back at school.

(O'Shea, 2015)

Introduction

The extensive quote above is from just one story vividly describing what Syrian families have gone through in their efforts to build a new life outside their devastated home country. It introduces the major theme of this chapter, which is the education of Syrian refugee children in Australia. This story is salutary evidence that refugee-background children are particularly differentiated by their experiences of violence and other traumatic events prior to arriving in Australia. The circumstances such children have personally been subjected to, or witnessed, include: war, bombing or shelling; destruction of homes and schools; violent death or injury of family or friends; separation from family members; sudden disappearances of family members or friends; physical injury and limited medical attention; being deprived of food, water and other resources; fear of discovery or arrest with subsequent detention or torture; forced conscription into armies or militias; rape or sexual assault; and lack of play opportunities. Ironically, Khaled's story above occurred in the context where Australia has a political climate and community debate that is generally concerned with ways to prevent refugees from reaching the country. For example, in 2016 the minister for immigration, Peter Dutton, claimed there was a link between refugee intakes and terrorism, suggesting that more refugees in the country would result in 'illiterate and innumerate' refugees either taking Australian jobs or living on government welfare (Song and Crealy, 2017).

The chapter examines Australian government policy responses and implementations with reference to refugee children, and the period after 2012 to the present day is particularly looked at. It was a period when the uptake of refugees, particularly from the Arabic-speaking world including Syria, Iraq and Afghanistan, increased. Analysed here is Australia's flagship refugee policy through the Refugee and Humanitarian Program and what this means for the education of affected children and especially Syrian ones who settle here. Given the influx of Syrian refugees into Australia following the events of 2011 in Syria, the following questions are asked:

1. How did the settlement and education policies for refugees change since 2012?
2. How did settlement policies affect the education policies for refugee children?
3. How did the settlement and education policies affect educational outcomes and integration of refugees into Australian society?

For many years the debate in Australia on refugee and asylum-seeker policy has become a very politicised, heated and emotional controversy. An increasingly important issue on the merits of refugees and asylum seekers, who represent one aspect of Australia's migrant intake, is the education of refugee children who reside in the country's cities and remote regions. It is evident that refugee children have greater educational and support needs compared to other newly arrived migrant students. Most refugee children and young people have experienced and, indeed, endured very disrupted lives and in many instances encountered poor or no education opportunities prior to their arrival in Australia. Furthermore, many have no literacy skills in their first language and face complex physical and mental health problems that are very much linked to their experiences. One media report in late 2017 found that refugee children encounter many challenges, due to current programmes and policies being 'piecemeal, unsystematic and have considerable gaps', often simply not realising students' unique needs (O'Keefe, 2017).

Refugees and asylum seekers in Australia: a summary

As the sixth largest country in the world and a continent all to itself, Australia has a total of nine states and territories spread over 7.6 million square kilometres. Australia is home to more than 25 million people, of whom more than one quarter were born overseas (Australian Bureau of Statistics, 2018). Since 1945, when the first Department of Immigration was established in Australia, about 7 million permanent migrants have settled in the country. The Department of Immigration and Citizenship has stated that the contribution of immigrants from all parts of the world to Australian society, culture and prosperity marked 'an important factor in shaping our nation' (Phillips et al., 2010). Yet, despite the fact that Australia is regularly described as a 'nation of immigrants', much confusion and misinformation exists in politics and the wider society regarding how many permanent migrants Australia has accepted over the decades. It is evident that publicly available statistics on both permanent and temporary migration are often used interchangeably and/or incorrectly. The consequence of this is that statistics employed to describe migration flows can be inaccurate or misleading. In terms of numbers, no official statistics were actually retained concerning refugee settlement from 1901 to 1948. Nonetheless, the Australian Parliamentary Library estimated that Australia during the July 1948 to June 1977 period received 269,266 assisted humanitarian arrivals. This was augmented by another 33,000 unassisted humanitarian arrivals. Since the Refugee and Humanitarian Program began operating in 1977, Australia has received 392,538 offshore refugee and humanitarian entrants and 42,714 onshore protection visas were issued (Refugee Council of Australia, 2012).

Australia's refugee programme had its origins dating back at least 170 years. In fact, the first group of refugees who can be identified were the Lutherans who settled in South Australia from 1839 onward, in order to flee the restrictions on their right to worship in Prussia. As the nineteenth century progressed other settlers such as the Hungarians, Poles and Italians left places where religious and political persecution were occurring. Following federation, the new Australian nation continued to permit refugees to arrive as unassisted migrants, the condition being that they had to meet restrictions set out in the Immigration (Restriction) Act 1901. This became the cornerstone of the 'White Australia' Policy. Small numbers of Greek, Russian, Armenian, Jewish, Bulgarian and Assyrian refugees were able to settle in Australia after proving they met the government's migration criteria. Between 1933 and 1939, more than 7,000 Jews escaped Nazi Germany and were settled. In 1937, the first refugee settlement support services were devised by the Australian Jewish Welfare Society with financial help from the Australian federal government. However, this settlement programme was cut short by the outbreak of World War II (Shoah Resource Center, n.d.; Rutland, 2005).

The post-war programme

Australia's Labor government in the immediate aftermath of World War II's cessation embarked on a much larger and ambitious refugee programme, the objective being to meet employment shortages in a growing economy and simply to increase the country's population ('populate or perish'). In July 1947, the Australian government entered into an agreement with the new International Refugee Organisation to settle displaced people from the camps in Europe. Subsequently, during the 1950s more than 170,000 refugees – the biggest groups being from Poland, Yugoslavia, Latvia, Lithuania, Estonia, Ukraine, Czechoslovakia and Hungary – were welcomed into the country. In order to meet the needs of refugees and other migrants, ship-board English classes were established (the precursor of the modern Adult Migrant English Program), army camps were turned into migrant hostels for on-arrival accommodation and the community-based strategy known as the Good Neighbour Council was established to foster and coordinate volunteer settlement support at the local level (Fleming, 1975). During the 1960s and early 1970s the overwhelming majority of refugees were Eastern Europeans escaping persecution in Soviet Bloc countries.

This was occurring at a time when the 'White Australia' policy was gradually breaking down and being shown to be redundant, given that Australian governments were increasingly trading with and entering into security alliances with Asian nations. The numbers of humanitarian arrivals increased substantially following the crushing of the Hungarian Revolution in 1956 and the Warsaw Pact countries' invasion of Czechoslovakia in August 1968. Interestingly enough, the refugee intake began to diversify in the early 1970s in the wake of the wars in Southeast Asia, and in 1972, when 198 Asians expelled by Uganda's then president Idi Amin were settled. Humanitarian settlement from Chile commenced the following year (1973) in the wake of the socialist Allende's government being overthrown by a military coup. Then in 1974, Cypriot refugees began arriving in Australia after the Turkish invasion of Northern Cyprus in 1974. This was followed shortly after by the 1975 hostilities in East Timor, bringing 2,500 evacuees to Darwin; it signalled the beginning of a Timorese refugee diaspora in Australia.

The collapse of the South Vietnamese government in Saigon in April 1975 started a chain of events which prompted the need to restructure Australia's refugee programme. Mass flights of Vietnamese refugees into nearby countries prompted an international response to which Australia committed support in the last year of the Whitlam government. By late 1975, the first 400 Vietnamese refugees were chosen by Australia for resettlement from camps in Hong Kong, Guam, Malaysia and Singapore. For the next two decades, Australia resettled more than 100,000 Vietnamese refugees from various Asian countries. Only a small proportion, around 2000, came directly to Australia by boat to seek asylum and during this time the term 'boat people' entered the Australian vernacular. Darwin received its first boat in April 1976 and on it were five Indochinese men. Over the next five years there were 2,059 Vietnamese boat arrivals with the last arriving in August 1981. The arrival of 27 Indochinese asylum seekers in November 1989 heralded the beginning of the second wave. Over the following nine years, boats arrived at the rate of about 300 people per year, and these mainly originated from Vietnam, Cambodia and southern China. In 1999 there was a third wave of asylum seekers, and these were predominantly from the Middle East; often in larger numbers than previous arrivals and usually with the assistance of 'people smugglers'.

These events make it clear that the scale of the refugee 'problem' was increasing as decade followed decade. Following the fall of Saigon in 1975, the Australian Senate's Standing Committee on Foreign Affairs and Defence was prompted to begin an investigation into how Australia should respond. In its 1976 report titled *Australia and the Refugee Problem*, the committee identified an urgent need for a new approach to refugee settlement. Citing the Department of Immigration's failure to offer any additional assistance to newly arrived Vietnamese refugees, the report said this provided 'irrefutable evidence of the complete lack of policy for the acceptance of people into Australia as refugees rather than as normal migrants'. The Senate committee made 44 recommendations concerning the need to develop a new refugee resettlement policy. This report marked the beginning of new thinking which changed the national refugee programme from the humanitarian element of a general migration programme, into one entailing a dedicated and planned humanitarian programme where settlement support would be more sophisticated.

Education of refugee children

Ideally, refugee children undertaking education in Australia should be enrolled in institutions that provide safe places for new encounters, learning opportunities and positive interactions. Essential to this is that classrooms deliver literacy and numeracy, viable post-school options, life choices, social and economic participation and a sense of settlement in the community. However, currently, Australian schools are poorly funded and ill-equipped to provide effective English as a second language (ESL) teaching and support. A few years ago the Refugee Council of Australia reported that people needing protection and coming to Australia are keen to study and begin training, in order to make up for lost time and opportunities, and young people especially are very motivated. Yet they encounter a myriad of problems in studying and training, especially if they arrive with little or no English and have had a very limited or different experience of education previously. Furthermore the council summarised the salient issues as follows (Refugee Council of Australia, 2016a):

- transitioning from life in refugee camps or a lengthy state of limbo;
- being put in classes by age and not their actual level of education;
- having to adjust to formal education for the first time;
- under pressure to begin employment to support themselves and/or their families;
- under-resourced public schools finding it a challenge to meet refugee students' needs;
- home environments that are difficult to live through because the process of settlement means family members cannot support them as much as they would like to; and
- experience of discrimination and racism in and outside the school.

In the early 1980s, the refugee programme grew to an annual intake of up to 22,000, the largest annual intake in 30 years. Vietnamese refugees settled from camps in Asia constituted the majority of new arrivals, with significant numbers of refugees also from Laos, Cambodia and Eastern Europe. They were augmented by smaller groups of Soviet Jews, Chileans, El Salvadorians, Cubans and members of ethnic minorities from Iraq, i.e. Assyrians, Chaldeans and Armenians. The Special Humanitarian Program began in 1981, providing a settlement option to people who had endured serious discrimination or human rights abuses, had escaped their country of origin and had close ties with Australia. In 1984, the refugee programme included 106 Ethiopians, the first significant group of Africans. During the mid-1980s as the Soviet system in Eastern Europe began to break down, the number of refugees and humanitarian entrants from Eastern Europe rose (Poland, Czechoslovakia, Hungary and Romania), the Middle East (Lebanon and Iran), Afghanistan, Sri Lanka, East Timor and Latin America (Chile and El Salvador). Awareness grew concerning the very real psychosocial impacts of persecution and conflict, leading in 1988 to the establishment of the first torture and trauma services in Sydney and Melbourne. In subsequent years, similar services were established in other state and territory capitals, resulting in the development of a national network of torture and trauma agencies.

Importantly, in 1989 a special visa category within the refugee programme was established to facilitate priority resettlement for refugee women at risk and their children. In the 20 years since then, under this programme Australian governments have resettled 8,800 refugee women and their children. In 1991, the Special Assistance Category (SAC) visa was introduced to respond to crises in particular countries, permitting settlement of people in vulnerable circumstances and with connections in Australia. The SAC offered resettlement options for people from the former Yugoslavia, the former Soviet Union, East Timor, Lebanon, Sudan, Burma, Vietnam, Sri Lanka and Cambodia and members of the Ahmadi religious movement. Gradually, however, the SAC was phased out by the Howard government, which expressed concern that it had, at least in part, become more of a family reunion programme. Its preference was for humanitarian family reunion to be handled under the Special Humanitarian Program, through the split family provisions it introduced from 1997.

The 1980s and 1990s were in fact decades that introduced significant changes to how settlement services were implemented, represented by the shift from migrant hostels to the On Arrival Accommodation programme, from the old Grant-in-Aid Program to the Community Settlement Services Scheme and with the replacement of the Community Resettlement Settlement Scheme in 1997 by the Integrated Humanitarian Settlement Strategy. The last decade has witnessed further changes to the provision of refugee services and significant shifts in the regional composition of the Refugee and Humanitarian Program. A decade ago, half of the programme was focused on resettlement from Europe. Now this makes up less than 1 percent of the programme. Resettlement from Africa increased from 16 to 70 percent in 2003–4 and 2004–5, being reduced to a third of the programme today. The continuing crisis in Iraq and the commencement of large-scale resettlement of Burmese from Thailand and Bhutanese from Nepal have seen the programme shift to one evenly divided between Africa, Asia and the Middle East.

Australian government policy on asylum seekers is complex and controversial, and continues to change. Australia has had a policy of mandatory detention for people arriving by boat without a valid visa since 1992, and indefinite immigration detention is possible under Australian law. Asylum seekers arriving by plane generally are not subject to mandatory detention, although this may apply if their visas are cancelled or expire. The offshore (people arriving from overseas) and onshore (people arriving in Australia and claiming asylum) components of Australia's Humanitarian Program have been linked since 1996. Thus an increase in onshore claims reduces the number of places for people arriving under the offshore programme, with significant effects on sponsored places for people in refugee-like situations (Royal Australasian College of Physicians, 2015).

The Australian Refugee and Humanitarian Program

Australia has had a long tradition of responding to humanitarian crises and resettling refugees and vulnerable people. It prides itself on providing the best settlement services and support to people in refugee and refugee-like situations (Department of Social Services, 2018a). Australia is a signatory to the UN 1951 Convention Relating to the Status of Refugees and the 1967 Protocol. These frame Australia's obligations to refugees, who include not only those coming into the country but also those living in offshore camps. Australia accepted the moral responsibility to coordinate with the UN's effort to respond to people in humanitarian crises. However, Australia reserves the right to set the targets in accepting humanitarian entrants and set in place objectives and mechanisms for ongoing humanitarian programmes (Australian Prime Ministers Centre, 2018; Koser, 2015). What Australian governments also consider is the capacity to assist.

The Refugee and Humanitarian Program is Australia's contribution and commitment to the international protection of refugees and refugee-like situations and to people seeking asylum. According to the Department of Home Affairs (2018a), the programme has been designed to ensure Australia's effective response to global humanitarian conditions and that support services are in place for entrants into the country. Compared to other refugee-receiving countries, the latest UNHCR report shows that Australia is placed third in providing permanent resettlement to refugees, next to Canada and the United States (Refugee Council of Australia, 2017). However, Australia received only 0.83 percent of the global share of new asylum seekers and recognised as refugees only 0.23 percent of the global total (Refugee Council of Australia, 2018). Clearly, based on these figures, Australia can do better in its acceptance of more humanitarian entrants in response to the refugee and asylum-seeking crises now occurring in many parts of the world. Only a handful of nations in Southeast Asia are signatories to the Refugee Convention and Australia is one of them. It is currently the case that the two main political parties, the centre-right Liberal/National Coalition and centre-left Labor, support a policy of turning back asylum-seeker boats at sea. This issue of 'turn-backs' has resulted in breaches of international law and, furthermore, a focus on deterring asylum seekers compromises the protection and promotion of human rights in the region (Dehm and Walden, 2018, pp. 593–5; Phillips, 2017).

In Australia, asylum is governed by various statutes and federal government policies aiming to implement Australia's obligations under the Convention Relating to the Status of Refugees, to which Australia is a party. Thousands of refugees have sought asylum in Australia since the end of World War II, and the major driving forces have been war, civil unrest, persecution and the Australian governments' desire for the country to have a larger population. From 1945 to the early 1990s, more than half a million refugees and other displaced persons were accepted into Australia (Gibney, 2004, p. 166). Historically, most asylum seekers arrived by plane but during the late 2000s and early 2010s, asylum seekers increasingly arrived by boat and this was received with some public disapproval (Phillips and Spinks, 2011). Asylum policy has now become a contentious 'wedge' issue in Australian politics, with the two major political parties in Australia arguing that the problem is a border-control issue and one concerning the safety of those attempting to reach Australia by boat.

Australia's Refugee and Humanitarian Program is administered by the Department of Home Affairs (2018a, 2018b). The Home Affairs Portfolio was established in December 2017, during which time the multicultural affairs function of the Department of Social Services was moved to the Department of Home Affairs. Implementing immigration and border policy functions previously held by the Department of Immigration and Border Protection is now under the Department of Home Affairs (2018c). The Australian Border Force, which protects Australia's borders and manages the movement of people and goods across the country, is an operationally independent body of the Department of Home Affairs (Newton,

2018). Overall, the programme consists of two permanent components: offshore (resettlement) and onshore (protection). Through the offshore component, resettlement is offered to people who have been found to be refugees or in refugee-like situations and who need protection and humanitarian assistance.

In 2012–13, it was announced that 20,000 places would have been allotted to humanitarian settlement of refugees in Australia, however, this figure declined with the change of government from Labor to Liberal in September 2013. Excluding the 12,000 people intake from Syria and Iraq in 2015, and the 13,750 humanitarian intakes from 2013 to 2017, this has been increased to 16,250 for 2017–18 and 18,750 for 2018–19 (Refugee Council of Australia, 2018; Department of Social Services, 2018b; Settlement Council of Australia, 2018). This is now referred to as a 'ceiling' to the Refugee and Humanitarian Program of Government. From November 2015 onward there was a steady stream of Syrian and Iraqi refugees coming in Australia and it continues to this day.

Recently, it was reported that Australia granted 13,770 humanitarian visas, fulfilling its obligation to protect refugees from persecution (Phillips, 2015; FindLaw Team, 2019). As at 11 December 2015, the number of Syrians who entered Australia as part of its Refugee and Special Humanitarian Program was 5,800 (Refugee Council of Australia, 2016c, p. 33). These people are processed outside Australia and they have been deemed unable to be repatriated or unable to integrate locally to their current host country. The UNHCR refers these cases to the Australian missions overseas. Self-referred applications may also be lodged. Refugee stream visas include the following: Refugee Visa (Subclass 200, 201, 203, 204) and Global Special Humanitarian (Subclass 202) (Migration Institute of Australia, 2015, p. 4).

The Offshore Humanitarian Program is mainly comprised of two streams: Refugee Program and the Special Humanitarian Program. The Refugee Program provides resettlement to Australia for refugees already outside their countries of origin and who are unable or unwilling to return to their home countries due to 'well-founded fear of persecution for reasons of race, religion, nationality, membership of a particular social group or political opinion' (UN Refugee Agency, 2018). The Special Humanitarian Program is aimed at refugees and asylum seekers. Regarding the onshore component, protection is provided to people who have come to Australia lawfully and who make a successful claim for asylum as assessed against the 1951 Refugee Convention. These people have either been considered as refugees, who have met the criteria for protection under the Migration Act of 1958 and are given a Permanent Protection Visa. Among the criteria that must be met for eligibility for a permanent protection visa are health, character requirements and security checks (Refugee Council of Australia, 2016b). Temporary Protection Visas (Subclass 866, 785), Temporary Humanitarian Stay (Subclass 449), Temporary Humanitarian Concern (Subclass 786) and Safe Haven Enterprise Visa (Subclass 790) may be offered to asylum seekers who arrive in Australia without a valid visa. They are, however, found to be in need of international protection.

Refugees holding these visas can be eligible for Specialised Intensive Services lasting for approximately five years after arrival to Australia or five years after their onshore visa has been granted (Spinks, 2009; Karlsen et al., 2011). All of these services are, however, subject to the approval of the Department of Social Services.

Australian education and refugee children

Schooling in Australia is compulsory in all Australian states and territories for children aged 6–16, from primary to secondary school years, regardless of background. As an overarching principle to Australian government education policies, federal or states and territories, the Australian Education Act 2013 was ratified and amended in 2018 and as such implemented as a framework for education providers (Australian Education Act, 2013). It acknowledges among other things that education is 'a foundation of a skilled workforce and creative community' and education playing a key role 'in overcoming social and economic disadvantage' (International Labour Organization, 2019). The Australian government, as a national policy leader for education, works with states and territories through the Council of Australian Governments and the Education Council. Education departments and authorities in the states and territories are required to deliver evidence-based reforms in schools. Commonwealth financial assistance for schools is provided in the Act to which states and territories are required, as a condition of financial assistance, to firstly comply with intergovernmental agreements on school education; and secondly implement nationally agreed policy initiatives on school education.

While the federal government provides funding to all Australian schools, government and non-government, state and territory governments are responsible for education policies. As such there are variations in their education systems and these are discussed elsewhere (Cooper, 2018, pp. 9–20; Matthews, 2008; McCarthy and Vickers, 2012). Some of the differences include age of compulsory schooling, curricular requirements and school year (grade) divisions. Public schools – also referred to as government schools – are tuition-free and accessible to all students who meet zoning preferences. Some government schools require fees that cover excursions, sporting and other in-school activities. Children from refugee backgrounds, except for those holding Temporary Visas, are afforded the same school fee privileges. School uniforms are required in most government and non-government schools (Education and Training Committee, 2007). The Australian curriculum has been developed to help all 'children in Australia to become successful learners, confident and creative individuals and active and informed citizens' (Australian Curriculum Assessment and Reporting Authority, 2014). Regardless of state and territory education policies and requirements, the curriculum provides the framework for what students should learn as they progress through their school life. It sets the learning goals and competencies from Foundation/Reception/Preparatory to Year 10. Major learning areas include English (and English as an additional language/dialect – EALD), mathematics, science, health and physical education, humanities and social sciences, arts, technologies and languages (Australian Curriculum Assessment and Reporting Authority, 2014).

As soon as possible, school-aged children of a humanitarian entrant are enrolled in government schools where the family residence is zoned. Schools are contacted by parents often with the help of service providers or case workers from migrant resource centres where the families are located (Australian Red Cross, 2019). Children from refugee backgrounds have access to high-quality schools and related services throughout Australia and they enjoy the same schooling privileges as local students. Their access to the Australian curriculum and support services is made available from both federal and state/territory governments as well as various non-government agencies catering to the education needs of refugee-background students. They have rights to non-discrimination on the basis of gender, race, colour, national or ethnic origin when accessing education and support mechanisms as provided (Australian Human Rights Commission, 2015). Under the multicultural education policy the Australian government is tied to the Australian Multicultural Advisory Council statement on cultural diversity and recommendations. This statement noted the enduring reality and necessity of multiculturalism to Australia. The policy is based on participation and inclusion that benefits all Australians (Koleth, 2010). Additionally, other supporting education policies have been enshrined in legislation to ensure that practical barriers to education are addressed (Blythe et al., 2018). Specialist government schools cater to students from refugee backgrounds and are regularly accessed from the time of their arrival and initial days spent in Australia, such as the School of Languages and the Secondary School of English. The School of Languages was founded to promote children's first-language maintenance and sustain interest in learning languages. Courses are offered from Reception to Year 12 and beyond the age of 18 for adult learners. The Adelaide Secondary School of English, for instance, educates students from culturally diverse backgrounds. Often some refugee students opt to come to the school to learn intensive English and eventually transition to other mainstream schools or participate in tertiary education or employment (Mackay et al., 2016).

Key concerns with the programmes and problems encountered by refugee students are outlined here. Some issues have been reflected in recent submissions to the Parliamentary Inquiry into Migrant Settlement Outcomes, which occurred in 2017 (Joint Standing Committee, 2017, pp. 57–62). The Australian Council of TESOL Associations (ACTA) has stated in regard to EALD programmes in Australia that: 'The major barrier to achieving educational excellence for EALD learners in Australian schools is the widespread, destructive impact of school autonomy and flexible resource management policies on targeted English language provision in schools' (2017, p. 1). Most of the concerns raised in submissions to the parliamentary Inquiry and individual reports by settlement organisations arose from the decentralisation of funding responsibility to the state and territory governments, and the responsibility put on schools to create and provide EALD programmes and training. However, greater autonomy is perceived by some schools to benefit refugee students because it allows increased flexibility to produce individualised programmes that can cater to the needs of an increasingly diverse student population. Furthermore, fluctuating funding can lead to a situation where long-term planning for students becomes problematic and unresolved, and may produce a situation where schools lack the skills to provide a cohesive and comprehensive programme (Joint Standing Committee, 2017, p. 59). Some schools and particularly those in regional areas may not be aware of the funding made available for EALD programmes (ACTA, 2017, pp. 4–5).

The rationale for the EALD programmes is that some children from non-English-speaking backgrounds take EALD classes. The EALD is a component of the Australian curriculum specifically developed to allow non-English-speaking and culturally and linguistically diverse students to equitably access Standard Australian English. As such, even students from migrant backgrounds and some Australian-born children and Aboriginal and Torres Strait Islander students, whose first language is not English, are able to access this English-language programme. In some states and territories, before joining mainstream schools, there are state government-run Schools of Languages that offer transition and support services for students whose first language is English and could barely communicate in English (School of Languages, 2018; Victorian School of Languages, 2018). Having diminished accountability for the type of programme and the progress made by students could give schools greater flexibility and could result in the misuse of allocated funding for EALD for other needs that are considered a higher priority (Joint Standing Committee, 2017, p. 60). Refugee children in Australia's schools require the expertise of properly trained EALD teachers, yet ACTA has noted the following (2017, p. 8): firstly, recognition of EALD qualifications is 'variable, lacking or unclear', due to it being a state and territory government responsibility; tertiary institutions are not providing EALD qualifications due to falling demand; many schools' efforts to enable further training for EALD teachers is not consistent with the gap in skill level of EALD teachers throughout Australia; and finally, decentralisation has led to falling EALD professional development support for teachers.

This is backed up by research on refugee children's education in Australia, which has concentrated for well over a decade on the challenges they face as well as their teachers (Cassity and Gow, 2005; Miller et al., 2005). As part of a large project on globalisation and refugee education in Queensland (Taylor, 2008; Matthews, 2008), research was undertaken in four Brisbane state high schools identified as having significant numbers of refugee students. In-depth interviews were conducted with ESL teachers, principals and deputy principals, liaison workers and guidance officers. The study's focus was on school policies and programmes concerning refugee students and it emerged that the teachers who were interviewed struggled to cope with the rising numbers and demands of their refugee students, who mainly arrived in Australia from various African countries. Not having enough resources simply resulted in shortages in ESL and general teaching staff, and in limited professional development which could well have helped them to meet the needs of refugee children more substantially. Most attention was given to language support and to social and emotional needs, meaning that less attention was being given to other learning requirements. Given that the ESL teachers were 'bearing the brunt' of more refugee students, it is not surprising that an emphasis on language support emerged. While it is true that community-sector workers can provide support for the refugee students' social and emotional needs of the refugees, problems such as these as evident in the Brisbane schools result from inadequate policies and their provision. As Sidhu and Taylor (2007, p. 283) have stated in their paper, the education of refugee children is being 'left to chance'.

The teachers interviewed were struggling to cope with the increased numbers and demands of their refugee students, who were mainly from various African countries (Taylor, 2008). Insufficient resources resulted in shortages in ESL and general teaching staff, and in limited professional development which might have assisted them to better meet the needs of refugees. Most attention was given to language support and to social and emotional needs, with less attention being given to other learning needs. Given that the ESL teachers were 'bearing the brunt' of the increased numbers of refugee students, it is not surprising that there was an emphasis on language support.

Community-sector workers provided support for the social and emotional needs of the refugees. These problems 'on the ground' in Brisbane schools seemed in part to be a result of the inadequacies in policy and provision: inadequacies which, it was claimed, led to the education of refugee students being 'left to chance' (Sidhu and Taylor, 2007). Much of the research on refugee education in Australia has focused on the challenges faced by refugee students and their teachers (Cassity and Gow, 2005; Miller et al., 2005). As part of a large project on globalisation and refugee education in Queensland (Taylor, 2008; Matthews, 2008), research was undertaken in four Brisbane state high schools identified as having significant numbers of refugee students. In-depth interviews were conducted with ESL teachers, principals/deputy principals, guidance officers and liaison workers. The focus of the study was on school policies and programmes concerning refugee students.

Children and adolescents from refugee backgrounds encounter significant educational disadvantages due to what they have experienced, the pressures and vicissitudes of migration and having to learn a new language. One Western Australian study on the education experience in refugee children (Mace et al., 2014) discovered that previous schooling was limited: two thirds of children, in fact, had their education interrupted, and only half the group experienced schooling in their first language, reflecting the complexity of their migration pathways. Paediatricians have for many years noted the interrupted education of refugee children entering under Australia's offshore programme; it has been reported that children missed out on months of school during their sojourn in Australian immigration detention (Corbett et al.,

2014). Refugees and asylum seekers should have equitable access to education at all life stages, with acknowledgement of prior interruption or limited access to education, and support for their right to attain their potential. While humanitarian entrants bring skills to Australia and New Zealand, the demographer Graeme Hugo does make the point that poor English proficiency is a significant impediment to workforce participation (Hugo, 2011). It has also in the last decade made it difficult for Syrian refugees to access services in Victoria (Paxton et al., 2011). In Australia, refugee arrivals with low English proficiency are entitled to English-language tuition to support settlement and entry into work or study (O'Dwyer and Mulder, 2015), whereas English-language tuition for asylum-seeker adults is extremely limited.

In Australia, refugee students' access and participation in the public education system has been compromised by poor transition strategies, with teachers feeling ill-equipped and not having enough resources to provide the required educational and psychosocial support for more refugee arrivals (Cassity and Gow, 2005; Miller et al., 2005). It has been claimed by Matthews that 'Australian schools are poorly funded and ill-equipped to provide effective English as a Second Language teaching and support' (2008, p. 31; see also Sidhu and Taylor, 2007). New South Wales receives about 40 percent of Australia's refugee intake, but it is reported that restricted resource allocations seriously compromise the amount of language and literacy support available to refugee students (Refugee Council of Australia, 2010, p. 40; Iredale and Fox, 1997, p. 655). There is a real need for increased mediation and reporting on students to ensure that long-term welfare, language and health needs are addressed throughout Australia (see Cassity and Gow, 2005, p. 55).

What was reported in western Sydney's Fairfield council area in 2017 reinforces the point that humanitarian migration to the area was not being resourced or funded, considering that the 4,975 Syrian/Iraqi refugees who arrived there in 2016 were followed by another 1,705 in the first half of 2017. The federal government had vowed to make sure that migrants integrated into the Australian community and learnt English, yet here was a good example of the local authorities having to tackle the problem, and they did so through the creation of the Fairfield City Settlement Action Plan with 50 service providers and community organisations. Unemployment in Fairfield stood at 9 percent and the federal government had effectively relocated 7,000 refugees (mainly Assyrians) to an area with little infrastructure and high unemployment. The manager of the Assyrian Resource Centre's community settlement services stated that English-language services were actually being funded by ClubGRANTS NSW, and the classes were supported by unpaid volunteers (Brennan, 2017).

Syrian refugee children in Australian schools – a snapshot

The results of a recent three-year project (the following is largely based on Collins et al., 2018) presented at a public seminar on 'Settlement Outcomes of Syrian-Conflict Refugee Families in Australia' focused on the education and employment of Syrians, and reference was made to the schooling of children. This particular project drew on the insights of important stakeholders working in this area, including policy makers, NGO representatives, employers and educators. Their report focused on what was happening in the three main states of settlement in Australia: New South Wales, Queensland and Victoria. Firstly, the great majority of Syrian-conflict refugees reported nil or poor levels of English, while most did not report their level of education. For those who did, the level of education greatly varied and the highest number of Iraqi and Syrian refugees had six years of schooling, followed by more advanced levels of education (p. 9). Focusing on pre-tertiary education and, specifically, the entrants to Australia arriving between 1 July 2015 and 31 December 2017, the statistics for Syrian children's level of schooling are as follows: 1 year (317); 2 years (323); 3 years (374); 4 years (369); 5 years (480); 6 years (1,355); 7 years (469); 8 years (552); 9 years (1,161); 10 years (231); 11 years (264); and 12 years (1,006) (p. 10). They have access to free public education like all other migrants who have permanent residency, and are provided with intensive language support with a focus on the families as a whole, particularly in the early years of settlement, i.e. the first one–five years (p. 22).

These children are living with their families in government-designated Humanitarian Settlement Program service provider locations, and organisations such as the Australian Red Cross Society, Settlement Services International, MDA, Melaleuca Refugee Centre and AMES Australia assist refugees with specialised services such as meeting clients at the airport, property induction (provision of information about tenancy rights and responsibilities, assistance with electricity modes, etc.), provision of an initial food package, assistance with registering and enrolling in institutions such as schools, banks, Medicare, Centrelink, Job Active and other key agencies, assistance with navigating the public transport system, connecting them with other community members and recreation programmes (p. 12).

Examples of the work that the states of New South Wales, Victoria and Queensland do for Syrian refugee children's schooling can be summarised here. In New South Wales students can attend the Beginning School Well programme to ensure their introduction to Australia's school system is smooth, and those in Years 8–12 can attend the Multicultural Playwright Program to develop creative writing skills and build friendships. The New South Wales Education Department established refugee teacher networks in Holroyd and Fairfield, and refugee support leader positions and refugee student support teams offering psychological expertise to schools, thereby assisting refugee students and their families. Intensive English centres are attached to high schools and specialist refugee support teachers take up a responsible role in enhancing education outcomes. In Victoria, the government initiative known as the Refugee Education Support Program has partnered with the Centre for Multicultural Youth and Foundation House in collaboration with Catholic Education Commission Victoria and Independent Schools Victoria. The objective here is to identify the gaps and implement solutions to support the education outcomes of refugee students, offering professional learning and consultation provided by school staff, out-of-school-hours care providers and volunteers. Referring to Queensland, funds have been allocated by the state government to the seven regions based on the number of 'weighted' refugees per region – the weightings are calculated on the number of refugees depending on how many years they have lived in Australia. Students are classified as being either 'New Arrivals', '1st year', '2nd year' or '3rd year' with most funding set aside for 'New Arrivals'. Funding can be used for language tuition, homework assistance, job preparation, counselling, interpreter services, intensive teaching or teacher aide support development. Again in Queensland, the Catholic Education Commission became very involved in young Syrian students' schooling, given that many of them are in fact Roman Catholic (Collins et al., 2018, pp. 22–3). As an example, St Francis College – a co-educational school in the southern Brisbane suburb of Crestmead – has set up art-therapy sessions for Syrian refugee students (Ng, 2018).

Possible future challenges and recommendations

It emerges in this chapter that Australia's education system is one where refugee children in various school grades face unique learning challenges. Given all the services and activities mentioned above, people from refugee backgrounds are provided with enough economic and social support to live in Australia. The future of people from refugee backgrounds seems bright due to the permanent settlement policies in place. However, the path to this status is significantly arduous and entrants are but a few in relation to the huge numbers of refugees requiring humanitarian support and settlement. Migrant and refugee children and families often feel isolated when they arrive in Australia and many children have experienced loss and trauma. Some struggle to adjust to life in a new country, where their social community and learning environments are very different to their country of origin. Federal and state government policies and initiatives can only succeed when family, cohesion, parental involvement and teachers having sensitivity about linguistic and cultural heritage are evident. Children from refugee backgrounds have often missed early detection opportunities and frequently have significant gaps in their prior schooling. Over a decade ago, but still very relevant today, Matthews (2008) noted that schools are a stabilising feature in the unsettled lives of refugee students, offering safe spaces for new encounters, interactions and learning opportunities. Literacy, which is the key to educational success, when taught effectively, will make possible post-school options, life choices, social participation and settlement.

On paper, the Australian Humanitarian Settlement Program and related policies that address the education and employment needs of refugees in general and student refugees in particular seem well entrenched, considering that Australia is a highly regarded destination of permanent settlement for refugees. Despite the fact that there are regular changes in the names of programmes and visas granted to refugee applicants to the country, as well as changes in government, the principle of permanently resettling refugees in Australia is a global obligation which Australia tries to meet as part of its commitment to the Refugee Convention. With the Humanitarian Settlement Program, Australia has reason to be proud of providing quality resettlement experiences to humanitarian entrants. A good anecdotal example of this that points the way to the future was documented a few years ago by Shrosbery (2016), writing about a Newcastle primary school's (Heaton Public School) successful intake of Syrian refugee students. To make their transition to Australian education and its possibilities worthwhile, the school employed learning-support officers, including an Arabic speaker, and built a new classroom for intensive language classes to accommodate the rising number of non-English speakers.

However, Australia can still do better in its intake of more refugees seeking resettlement. Referring to the Syrian refugee intake specially, the Refugee Council of Australia recommended that the Australian government make extra resettlement commitments of 10,000 places each year for the next three years, but also that this responsibility be adequately resourced (Refugee Council of Australia, 2016c, pp. 8, 52). The settlement policies likewise set provisions for refugee education, albeit the states and territories have free agency to design their own policies and procedures. While refugee education policies developed by each state or territory seem to provide support services to refugee students and some degree of success is claimed in improving educational outcomes for students, it remains to be seen whether these programmes and provisions work for particular refugee communities. Furthermore, such schemes can only work if they are not subsumed under a 'one-size-fits-all' state policy for refugee education. Added to this, it has been reported that access to education and English-language classes continue to be a major issue. The Refugee Council of Australia (2016c, p. 6) states that the introduction of Temporary Protection Visas has effectively denied access to further education to people currently seeking asylum who arrived by boat, because of the requirement that they pay international student fees. This compounds existing difficulties, such as the ability to attend high school after the age of 18, added to the stress of seeking asylum inhibiting engagement with schools. Very recently, service providers also reported that, under the new Status Resolution Support Services programme, more people failed to qualify, with the burden falling on organisations that had to operate without government funding. Further, the new programme involves large and complex caseloads that are underfunded and provide only for very limited client contact, jeopardising the health and well-being of both people seeking asylum and the staff of service providers (Williams, 2018).

Currently, Australian schools are poorly funded and ill-equipped to provide effective ESL teaching and support. A new cohort of refugee students mainly from Africa and the Middle East are struggling. For children from a refugee or asylum-seeking background, entering an Australian school is an enormous change that tends to involve learning an additional language and adapting to new expectations, routines, assumptions, presumptions and cultural attitudes and norms. These challenges make it difficult for educators to detect learning problems early enough to provide appropriate support mechanisms. Children arrive in Australia – and other countries, it should not be forgotten – with a wealth of experience and represent different cultures and perspectives which can greatly enhance the classrooms into which they arrive. However, the reality is that there is no evidence on the best education approaches that can support pre-school, primary and secondary school children to recover from past trauma.

Education is an essential aspect of settlement and it is increasingly recognised that education and schools support the health and well-being of refugee children, and furthermore, English-language tuition is valuable for new arrivals with low English proficiency. More broadly, the motivation and potential demonstrated by many children and people of refugee backgrounds 'provides a compelling argument for developing more innovative and flexible strategies for participation in education' (Correa-Velez et al., 2010, cited in Royal Australasian College of Physicians, 2015, p. 17). Specific support is required to ensure students of refugee background reach their full educational and social potential, and this study makes it clear that Australia does have multiple strategies in place to support refugee school students. All children in Australia have a right to education. Under the Convention on the Rights of the Child, Australian governments are required to provide, as a minimum, primary education that is 'compulsory and available free to all' and secondary education that is 'available and accessible to every child'.

Within refugee programming in Australian schools, there needs to be continued and ongoing case management for refugee students so as to prevent vulnerable students from 'falling through the gaps'. Refugee youth have a propensity to be lost and/or neglected after their initial transition into mainstream schooling, and accordingly, ongoing follow-up and support is imperative. Additionally, this extra support may prevent students from falling behind in subjects, failing to understand school expectations and/or struggling to make meaningful social connections in their school and/or the wider community. Refugees as high-need students must be recognised and assisted as a discrete population, with targeted funding for assistance programmes. In several Australian states, non-targeted funding for ESL and/or special needs means these services do not have guaranteed monetary support. It is therefore important that the needs of the student population are reflected in funding for specialist educational programmes, resources and staffing.

A future challenge for Australia is the requirement for more government-supported, community-based initiatives to promote the education and active involvement of refugees in Australia's urban and regional centres. Refugee populations are often settled within disadvantaged urban areas and accordingly can become affiliated with and/or conflated into other disadvantaged youth groups. As Creary (2015, p. 16) has suggested, there is scope for alternative public and/or subsidised housing solutions. The wider mobilisation of volunteers in the community is significant to this end. Residents often invest in assisting the youth of their own community, and this investment should be utilised through the provision of forums and programmes across Australia where volunteers can get involved. In the current political environment, many people are in fact altruistically motivated to help refugees in some small way and have a positive impact on the lives of displaced people, such as the Syrians. This groundswell should be targeted through effective programmes established to assist in integration, language acquisition and a deeper understanding of services, such as the school system.

Community-based programmes centred on developing leaders from within migrant and refugee communities are vital. This helps to bridge gaps in understanding and cultural differences as well as allow individuals to remain connected to their heritage. Ultimately, fostering strong links between communities will benefit refugee youth and bridge their experiences within two differing cultures. It must be acknowledged that the act of migration – including the arrival of refugees – changes the demography of the nation. Over the last few decades, Australia has changed markedly and, accordingly, services and social/educational perspectives must be adapted to the needs of these new Australians. Institutional adaptation is essential because if there is no institutional flexibility, then ultimately no adequate addressing of shifting needs will be met.

School-wide curriculum must be re-examined by policy makers and educators to develop approaches to refugee education that recognise the special needs of Syrian refugee students. Australian schools must ensure that they are provided with sufficient tools to transfer their knowledge or, alternatively, to gain the skills they missed out on prior to arrival in their host country. Failing to do so will create difficulties for learners and teachers, and may furthermore compound the refugee's feeling of being educationally devalued. Currently, there are ongoing curriculum debates in Australia concerning teacher specialisation and training in ESL, as well as the provision of resources within Australian schools (Jones and Chen, 2012; Paolino, 2012, pp. 260–1). Australia's neoliberal political environment, which has been a reality of life now for nearly 30 years and to some extent dictates federal and state/territory government policies, has resulted in governments withdrawing resources from the public school system, whilst obligations are simultaneously placed on schools by federal departments in the form of standardised testing. Accurate benchmarking of special needs and ESL students cannot purely be addressed by a standardised test, so a realistically moderated and modified form of benchmarking for refugee students should be put in place.

This chapter has described in detail what policy makers and Australia's government can do to help refugee children to thrive in school, and where possible, with reference to the Syrian refugee children intake (Maadad, 2019). The following recommendations are made with the aim of making an important and life-long difference to refugee children's learning experiences:

- Refugees and asylum seekers should have equitable access to education at all stages of life, with acknowledgement of prior interruption or limited access to education.
- Establish a coordinated whole-school response for supporting refugee students and their individual needs.
- Ensure that effective school enrolment and orientation processes are available so that refugee students can be identified and supported in their transition to school.
- Implement school policies and practices that are effective in identifying and addressing the needs of refugee students.
- Allocate resources which target the relevant educational, physical, social and emotional well-being factors of refugee students, with proper access to counselling resources, and support for bilingual and EALD students.
- Include refugee student-support strategies as a critical aspect of school plans.
- Ensure the collection and maintenance of accurate data on refugee students, their needs and what progress they are making in their learning.
- Make sure that data on the well-being and educational needs of refugee students inform the development of personalised learning-support approaches.
- Ensure that schools' staff understand the impact of trauma and can respond well to the learning and welfare needs of refugee students.
- Work with appropriate agencies to support newly arrived refugee students and their families.

If these recommendations are implemented on a nationwide basis, with close agreement between the federal and state governments, and particularly where there is good coordination between departments or agencies and the actual education institutions, it is very likely that refugee children can realise the resilience they bring with them to Australia.

References

Australian Bureau of Statistics (2018). Population Clock. Retrieved 20 July 2018 from www.abs.gov.au/ausstats/abs@.nsf/Web+Pages/Population+Clock?opendocument.

Australian Council of TESOL Associations (2017). 'Submission to the Review to Achieve Educational Excellence in Australian Schools'. Retrieved 7 January 2019, from http://tesol.org.au/.

Australian Curriculum Assessment and Reporting Authority (2014). 'Australian Curriculum Overview: Learning Areas'. Retrieved 12 June 2018 from www.australiancurriculum.edu.au/f-10-curriculum/learning-areas/.

Australian Education Act (2013). No. 67, 2013 Stat. (Office of Parliamentary Counsel, Canberra 2018).

Australian Government Department of Home Affairs (2017). 'Australia's Offshore Humanitarian Program: 2016–2017'. Canberra: Commonwealth of Australia.

Australian Government Department of Home Affairs (2018a). 'Humanitarian Settlement Program'. Retrieved 12 June 2018 from www.dss.gov.au/settlement-services/programs-policy/settlement-services/humanitarian-settlement-program.

Australian Government Department of Home Affairs (2018b). 'Fact Sheet: Australia's Refugee and Humanitarian Program'. Retrieved 30 June 2018 from www.homeaffairs.gov.au/about/corporate/information/fact-sheets/60refugee.

Australian Government Department of Home Affairs (2018c). 'Our History'. Retrieved 15 July 2018 from www.homeaffairs.gov.au/about/corporate/history.

Australian Human Rights Commission (2015). 'Rights to Equality and Non Discrimination'. Retrieved 7 January 2019 from www.humanrights.gov.au/rights-equality-and-non-discrimination.

Australian Prime Ministers Centre (2018). 'Australia's Refugee Policy'. Press release. Retrieved 7 January 2019 from static.moadoph.gov.au/ophgovau/media/images/apmc/docs/81-Refugees.pdf.

Australian Red Cross (2019). 'Help for Migrants in Transition'. Retrieved 10 January 2019 from www.redcross.org.au/get-help/help-for-migrants-in-transition/visit-a-hub.

Blythe, R., Clarke, J., Connell, T., Wallace, J. and Wood, C. (2018). *States of Refuge: Access to Health, Housing and Education for People Seeking Asylum and Refugees in Australia.* Melbourne: Liberty Victoria's Rights Advocacy Project.

Brennan, Rose (2017). 'Fairfield Council Say They Are Lacking Resources, Funds, Jobs to Integrate Thousands of Refugees'. *Daily Telegraph,* 26 June. Retrieved from www.dailytelegraph.com.au/projectsydney/fairfield-council-complaining-they-are-lacking-resources-funds-jobs-to-integrate-thousands-of-refugees/news-story/ade9c7da39c8dc67365f5d5b26fef4b1.

Cassity, E. and Gow, G. (2005). 'Shifting Space and Cultural Place: The Transition Experiences of African Young People in West Sydney Schools'. Paper presented at the Australian Association of Educational Research, Annual Conference, Sydney.

Collins, J., Reid, C., Groutsis, D., Ozkul, D. and Watson, K. (2018). 'Report: Syrian-Conflict Refugee Settlement in Australia'. Public Seminar on Responses to Syrian-Conflict Refugee Settlement in Australia, Germany, Sweden, Finland, UK, Canada and New Zealand, 12–14 March.

Cooper, Madeleine (2018). 'Education Pathways for Refugee and Migrant Youth'. Prepared for the Settlement Council of Australia.

Corbett, E.J.M., Gunasekera, H., Maycock, A. and Isaacs, D. (2014). 'Australia's Treatment of Refugee and Asylum Seeker Children: The Views of Australian Paediatricians'. *Medical Journal of Australia,* 201(7), 393–398. doi: doi:10.5694/mja14.00279.

Crealy, Isobel Rose (2015). The Peter Mitchell Churchill Fellowship to Investigate Language and Cultural Inclusion Programs Illustrating Best Practice in the Integration of Adolescent Refugee Students – Canada, USA. The Winston Churchill Memorial Trust of Australia.

Dehm, Sara and Walden, Max (2018). 'Refugee Policy: A Cruel Bipartisanship'. In Anika Gauja, Peter Chen, Jennifer Curtin and Juliet Pietsch (eds), *Double Disillusion: The 2016 Australian Federal Election* (pp. 593–617). Canberra: ANU Press.

Department of Social Services (2018a). 'Government Support'. Retrieved 12 June 2018 from www.dss.gov.au/settlement-services/helping-refugees/get-involved/government-support.

Department of Social Services (2018b). 'Settlement Services'. Retrieved 7 January 2019 from www.dss.gov.au/settlement-services-programs-policy/syrian-iraqi-humanitarian-crisis.

Education and Training Committee (2007). 'Final Report: Inquiry into Dress Codes and School Uniforms in Victorian Schools'. Retrieved 10 January 2019 from www.parliament.vic.gov.au/archive/etc/reports/schooluniform/execsum&recs.pdf.

FindLaw Team (2019). 'What Are the Types of Humanitarian Visas Available in Australia?'. *FindLaw Australia*. Retrieved 3 January 2019 from www.findlaw.com.au/articles/4303/what-are-the-types-of-humanitarian-visas-available.aspx

Fleming, C.I. (1975). *A History of the Good Neighbour Council of the Australian Capital Territory Inc.* Canberra: Good Neighbour Council of the A.C.T.

Gibney, Matthew (2004). *The Ethics and Politics of Asylum: Liberal Democracy and the Response to Refugees*. Cambridge: Cambridge University Press.

Hugo, G. (2011). 'Economic, Social and Civic Contributions of First and Second Generation Humanitarian Entrants'. Adelaide: National Centre for Social Applications of Geographical Information Systems, University of Adelaide, 30 July. Retrieved 26 February 2019 from www.immi.gov.au/media/publications/research/_pdf/ economic-social-civic-contributions-about-the-research2011.pdf.

International Labour Organization (2019). 'A Skilled Workforce for Strong, Sustainable and Balanced Growth'. Retrieved 18 February 2019 from www.ilo.org/skills/pubs/WCMS_151966/lang–en/index.htm.

Iredale, Robyn and Fox, Christine (1997). 'The Impact of Immigration on School Education in New South Wales, Australia'. *International Migration Review*, 31(3), 655–669.

Joint Standing Committee on Migration (2017). 'Inquiry into Migrant Settlement Outcomes'. Canberra: Parliament of Australia.

Jones, P.T. and Chen, H. (2012). 'Teachers' Knowledge about Language: Issues of Pedagogy and Expertise'. *Australian Journal of Language and Literacy*, 35(2), 147–168.

Karlsen, Elibritt, Phillips, Janet and Koleth, Elsa (2011). 'Seeking Asylum: Australia's Humanitarian Program'. Parliament of Australia, Department of Parliamentary Services.

Koleth, Elsa (2010). 'Multiculturalism: A Review of Australian Policy Statements and Recent Debates in Australia and Overseas'. Research Paper no. 6 2010–2011. Parliament of Australia, Social Policy Section.

Koser, Khalid (2015). 'Australia and the 1951 Refugee Convention'. Lowy Institute, 30 April. Retrieved 3 January 2019 from www.lowyinstitute.org/publications/australia-and-1951-refugee-convention.

Maadad, N. (2019). Research project with Centre of Lebanese Studies funded by Spencer Foundation. www.spencer.org/towards-inclusive-education-refugees-comparative-longitudinal-study.

Mace, A.O., Mulheron, S., Jones, C. and CherianS. (2014). 'Educational, Developmental and Psychological Outcomes of Resettled Refugee Children in Western Australia: A Review of School of Special Educational Needs: Medical and Mental Health Input'. *Journal of Paediatrics and Child Health*, 50(1), 985–992.

Mackay, K., Moustakim, M., Mupenzi, A. and Mar, P. (2016). 'Navigating Resettlement Report'. University of Western Sydney. Retrieved 4 January 2019 from www.sydwestms.org.au/images/documents/Navigating-Resettlement-Report-updated-030718-2.pdf.

Matthews, J.M. (2008). 'Schooling and Settlement: Refugee Education in Australia'. *International Studies in Sociology of Education*, 18(1), 31–45.

McCarthy, F.E. and Vickers, M.H. (2012). 'Australia's New Arrivals Policy and the Need to Reform Refugee Education Provision'. In F.E. McCarthy and M.H. Vickers (eds), *Refugee and Immigrant Students: Achieving Equity in Education* (pp. 145–165). Charlotte, NC: Information Age Publications.

Migration Institute of Australia (2015). 'Submission: Offshore Refugee and Humanitarian Visas: Creating a Simpler Framework'. NSW/ACT Branch.

Miller, J., Mitchell, J. and Brown, J. (2005). 'African Refugees with Interrupted Schooling in the High School Mainstream: Dilemmas for Teachers'. *Prospect*, 20(2), 19–33.

Newton, Mandy (2018). 'The Australian Border Force'. *United Service*, 69(2), 21–24.

Ng, Emilie (2018). 'Syrian and Iraqi Refugees who Escaped War Find Healing through Art Teacher's Therapy Session'. *Catholic Leader*, 1 March. Retrieved 27 February 2019 from http://catholicleader.com.au/news/syrian-iraqi-refugees-escaped-war-find-healing-art-teachers-therapy-session.

O'Dwyer, M. and Mulder, S. (2015). *Finding Satisfying Work: The Experiences of Recent Migrants with Low Level English*. Melbourne: AMES Australia, Research and Policy Unit.

O'Keefe, D. (2017). 'Refugee Students Need More Support: Study Finds'. *Australian*, 5 December. Retrieved 21 August 2018 from www.theaustralian.com.au/higher-education/refugee-students-need-more-support-study-finds/news-story/80920005ede26075232a0287f40a329e.

O'Shea, David (2015). 'Syrian Boy Horrifically Maimed in Aleppo Shelling Starts New Life in Wollongong, Australia'. *ABC News*, 16 September. Retrieved 3 January 2019 from www.abc.net.au/news/2015-09-16/boy-horrifically-maimed-in-syria-starts-new-life-in-wollongong/6780582.

Paolino, A. (2012). *An Interdisciplinary Intervention: The Potential of the Orff-Schulwerk Approach as a Pedagogical Tool for the Effective Teaching of Italian to Upper Primary Students in Western Australia*. Thesis, Edith Cowan University. Retrieved 4 January 2019 from https://ro.ecu.edu.au/cgi/viewcontent.cgi?referer=https://www.google.com.au/&httpsredir=1&article=1558&context=theses.

Paxton, G.A., Smith, N., Win, A.K., Mulholland, N. and Hood, S. (2011). *Refugee Status Report: A Report on How Refugee Children and Young People in Victoria Are Faring*. Melbourne: Victorian Government, Department of Education and Early Childhood Development. Retrieved 26 February 2019 from www.education.vic.gov.au/Documents/about/research/refugeestatusreport.pdf.

Phillips, Janet (2015). 'Asylum Seekers and Refugees: What Are the Facts?' Parliament of Australia, Social Policy Section. Retrieved 3 January 2019 from www.aph.gov.au/About_Parliament/Parliamentary_Departments/Parliamentary_Library/pubs/rp/rp1415/AsylumFacts.

Phillips, Janet (2017). 'A Comparison of Coalition and Labor Government Asylum Policies in Australia since 2001'. Parliament of Australia, Social Policy Section. Retrieved 3 January 2019 from www.aph.gov.au/About_Parliament/Parliamentary_Departments/Parliamentary_Library/pubs/rp/rp1617/AsylumPolicies.

Phillips, Janet and Harriet Spinks (2011). 'Boat Arrivals in Australia since 1976'. *Background Notes*, 5 January. Commonwealth of Australia. Retrieved 16 August 2018 from www.aph.gov.au/About_Parliament/Parliamentary_Departments/Parliamentary_Library/pubs/BN/2012-2013/BoatArrivals.

Phillips, Janet, Klapdor, Michael and Simon-Davies, J. (2010). 'Migration to Australia since Federation: A Guide to the Statistics'. Parliament of Australia. Retrieved 17 August 2018 from www.aph.gov.au/About_Parliament/Parliamentary_Departments/Parliamentary_Library/pubs/BN/1011/MigrationPopulation.

Refugee Council of Australia (2010) 'Finding the Right Time and Place: Exploring Post-Compulsory Education and Training Pathways for Young People from Refugee

Backgrounds in NSW'. Retrieved 16 August 2018 from www.refugeecouncil.org.au/r/rpt/2010-Education.pdf.

Refugee Council of Australia (2012). 'History of Australia's Refugee Program'. Retrieved 16 August 2018 from www.refugeecouncil.org.au/getfacts/seekingsafety/refugee-humanitarian-program/history-australias-refugee-program/.

Refugee Council of Australia (2016a). 'Education and Training'. Retrieved 21 August 2018 from www.refugeecouncil.org.au/getfacts/settlement/learninghere/education-and-training/

Refugee Council of Australia (2016b). 'How Australia Determines if a Person Is a Refugee'. Retrieved 12 June 2018 from www.refugeecouncil.org.au/getfacts/seekingsafety/asylum/australia-determines-person-refugee/.

Refugee Council of Australia (2016c). 'Australia's Response to a World in Crisis: Community Views on the 2016–17 Humanitarian Program'. Retrieved 12 June 2018 from www.refugeecouncil.org.au/wp-content/uploads/2018/01/Australias-response-to-a-world-in-crisis_2016_2017.pdf.

Refugee Council of Australia (2017). 'UNHCR Global Trends 2016: How Australia Compares with the World'. Retrieved 12 June 2018 from www.refugeecouncil.org.au/getfacts/statistics/intl/unhcr-global-trends-2016-australia-compares-world/.

Refugee Council of Australia (2018). 'Recent Changes in Australian Refugee Policy'. Retrieved 10 July 2018 from www.refugeecouncil.org.au/publications/recent-changes-australian-refugee-policy/.

Refugee Council of Australia (n.d.). 'Australia's Refugee and Humanitarian Program'. Retrieved 16 August 2018 from www.refugeecouncil.org.au/refugee-humanitarian-program/.

Royal Australasian College of Physicians (2015). *Policy on Refugee and Asylum Seeker Health*. Sydney. Retrieved 21 August 2018 from www.racp.edu.au/docs/default-source/advocacy-library/policy-on-refugee-and-asylum-seeker-health.pdf?sfvrsn=6b092f1a_0.

Rutland, Susan (2005). *The Jews in Australia*. Port Melbourne: Cambridge University Press.

School of Languages (2018). 'Languages'. Retrieved 12 July 2018 from https://schooloflanguages.sa.edu.au/languages/.

Settlement Council of Australia (2018). *Fundamentals of Effective Settlement*. Deakin, ACT: SCOA.

Shoah Resource Center (n.d.). 'Australia, Jewish Refugees In'. *Yad Veshem*. Retrieved 3 January 2019 from www.yadvashem.org/odot_pdf/Microsoft%20Word%20-%205787.pdf.

Shrosbery, Karen (2016). 'Schools Welcoming Syrian Refugee Children Well Prepared to Help Them Settle In'. *ABC News*, 7 November. Retrieved 4 January 2019 from www.abc.net.au/news/2016-11-07/syrian-refugees-start-first-day-at-school-in-australia/7988884.

Sidhu, R. and Taylor, S. (2007). 'Educational Provision for Refugee Youth in Australia: Left to Chance?' *Journal of Sociology*, 43(3), 283–300.

Song, Jay and Crealy, Isobel (2017). 'Why Teaching Refugee Children Is so Critical'. *Interpreter*. Lowy Institute, 18 January. Retrieved 4 January 2019 from www.lowyinstitute.org/the-interpreter/why-teaching-refugee-children-so-critical.

Spinks, Harriet (2009). 'Australia's Settlement Services for Migrants and Refugees'. Research Paper no. 29 2008–2009. Parliament of Australia, Social Policy Section. Retrieved 3 January 2009 from www.aph.gov.au/About_Parliament/Parliamentary_Departments/Parliamentary_Library/pubs/rp/rp0809/09rp29.

Taylor, Sandra C. (2008). 'Schooling and the Settlement of Refugee Young People in Queensland: "… the Challenges Are Massive"'. *Social Alternatives*, 27(3), 58–65.

UN Refugee Agency (2018). *The 1951 Refugee Convention*. Retrieved 12 June 2018 from www.unhcr.org/en-au/3b66c2aa10.

Victorian School of Languages (2018). 'VSL: Victoria's Leading Language School'. Retrieved 12 July, 2018, from www.vsl.vic.edu.au/.

Williams, Wendy (2018). 'Alarm as Government Begins Cuts to Asylum Seeker Support Services'. *Probono Australia*, 27 June. Retrieved 4 January 2019 from https://probonoaustralia.com.au/.

5
POLICIES AND EDUCATION FOR REFUGEES IN SWEDEN

> The vast majority of children are peaceful, scared and desperate to start a new life. They are the type that Save the Children talks about. But, as Sweden has found, there are many kinds of child refugees. There are fake children, who lie about their age to have a better chance of asylum. There are 'anchor children', who are sent ahead by their desperate family. There are also trafficked children, who may still be in the hands of gangmasters and are being forced into work or prostitution. And there are the 'street children' who live in abandoned buildings and are often sucked into a criminal underworld. In Gothenburg recently, 18 boys were found in an abandoned house with no toilets and no heating; the temperature was well below zero. They were sleeping on the floor, many under the same quilt to keep warm – one was just nine years old. But after being placed in a care home, they ran away and ended up sleeping rough again.
>
> *(Nelson, 2016)*

Introduction

The long statement above is from an article by Fraser Nelson, writing for the United Kingdom newspaper the *Telegraph* in late January 2016. It vividly and sadly describes the plight of refugee children living in Stockholm, the capital city of Sweden, which the author had once lauded as a veritable shining and civilised beacon of how those facing desperate straits should be treated. The description above, however, illustrates what goes tragically and graphically wrong when welcoming more migrants than can be looked after. This chapter discusses the education experiences, opportunities and outcomes for Syrian refugee children in Sweden. Sweden emerges as an important case study because in recent years it has – compared to other European Union (EU) states – become one of the largest receiving countries not only of refugee children, but of minors who are *unaccompanied* by either parent or legal guardian. Crul (n.d., p. 4) writes that Sweden has received many more unaccompanied minors than other countries.

On the issue of refugee children and their schooling, one recent report on Sweden stated: 'the ambition is to give refugee pupils an equal chance to reach school outcomes at par with children of native descent ... also for refugee children ... the aim should be to reach higher education' (Crul, 2017, p. 4). Recently, it was stated (Fratzke, 2017, p. 3) that: 'Sweden has long had one of the most efficient and generous asylum systems in the world. The country has been lauded for and taken great pride in the high quality of care it provides to refugees and others in need of protection.'

Seemingly, this vision of Sweden as a consistent and generous 'safe haven' for refugees and their children was evident at the end of September 2015, when its government announced an extra $3 billion to its national budget to address education and housing issues and to restore a welfare system that had been under pressure in recent years. Between 2012 and 2014, Sweden received 55,210 Syrian asylum claims and this was topped only by Germany with 61,885 claims. There had in fact been a substantial rise in the number of claims from Syrians during this time: 7, 920 in 2012; 16,540 in 2013; and 30,750 in 2014 (Ostrand, 2015, p. 269). However, Sweden witnessed an unprecedented number of 6,901 people seeking asylum in just one week – 3,467 of them from Syria (Faughey, 2015). These were part of the then current estimated figure, i.e. 74,000 for asylum applications into Sweden (Johnson and Sennero, 2015). Furthermore, according to Faughey (2015):

> Local authorities will get more than 1 billion crowns extra for integrating refugees this year, with government also increasing spending to support refugee children in school. Total spending on refugees will rise to 19.4 billion crowns in 2016 out of a total budget of around 920 billion and up from an estimated 17.4 billion this year.

This changed in the wake of the Swedish prime minister Stefan Löfven and deputy prime minister Åsa Romson announcing in November 2015 that the country could no longer receive further asylum seekers (Berg, 2016; Fratzke, 2017, p. 3). Instead, a much more restrictive system of asylum and border-control measures would be enacted to stem the flow of new arrivals (Crouch, 2015). The nearly 163,0000 asylum applications received by Sweden in 2015 overwhelmed its ability to cope with this flow, prompting significant legislative changes to reduce its protective commitments (BBC News, 2016; Berg, 2016; Bunar, 2017, p. 3; EMN, 2016). Briefly, the 'human face' of a struggling asylum-seeker system was documented by one researcher who went to Malmo and interacted with a group of Syrian refugees aged 19–23 on a government chartered bus ride to northern Sweden. There was a 'breakdown in communication' about their rights to immediate employment, which these Syrians did not know about, and they were being sent to shelters in rural northern Swedish towns where they had to stay until they received the appropriate documentation enabling them to work (Mahmoud, 2016, pp. 25–6).

Sweden did experience a rapid rise in the numbers of unaccompanied refugee children seeking asylum there. For example, during the first two weeks of October 2015 alone, well over 4,000 unaccompanied minors arrived in Sweden, bringing the total of that year to 18,000, which was more than 2.5 times than the 7,000 who arrived during the whole of 2014 (sa/ks, 2015). Sweden in 2015 became in fact the most popular destination for refugee children travelling alone to Europe, and it received nearly a third of all unaccompanied minors. Again with reference to statistics, nearly 40,000 unaccompanied minors – who were largely boys aged between 13 and 18 – were expected to apply for asylum in Europe, according to the Swedish Migration Agency (sa/ks, 2015). It is important to note here that children under the age of 18 and who are outside their country of origin and separated from both parents and/or legal/customary caregiver are defined as unaccompanied minors/separated children. Unaccompanied minors arrive predominantly as asylum seekers in Sweden instead of through other channels (Çelikaksoy and Wadensjö, 2015a, pp. 2–3).

Statistical context

Having approximately 10 million inhabitants, Sweden is a relatively small country but famous for its generous welfare system. The country was similarly renowned for its liberal migration policy towards asylum seekers and refugees, to the extent that resettled refugees in Sweden received a permanent residence permit (Ostrand, 2015, p. 268, f. 43). When Sweden in 2015 received the aforementioned 163,000 refugees who originated from Syria, Iraq and Afghanistan, approximately 70,000 of them were minors under the age of 18 years. It has been estimated that nearly 35,000 were unaccompanied children, primarily from Afghanistan (Bunar, 2017, p. 3). When tighter border controls throughout Europe were set up and stricter refugee admission policies were implemented in Sweden, the Swedish Migration Agency reported that this number fell to 30,000 refugees in 2016, of which 10,000 were children (p. 3).

To establish the context of this chapter's analysis of refugee/asylum-seeking children in Sweden, the country had the third highest number of asylum claims in the EU from 2013 to 2015, and Sweden registered the greatest number of asylum claims by unaccompanied children in 2013 and 2014 (Çelikaksoy and Wadensjö, 2015a, p. 4). One study has suggested that between 2015 and 2018, approximately 220,000 refugees have been received into Sweden (Mangrio et al., 2018). The European Migration Network in its 2016 country factsheet for Sweden reported that for that year, Sweden documented the lowest annual figure of asylum seekers – 28,939 people applied for asylum – since 2009 (EMN,

2016, p. 1). Due to changes in the Reception of Asylum Seekers Act which entered into force on 1 June 2016, a person who applied for asylum and received a final refusal of entry or expulsion order could no longer claim accommodation and daily allowances provided by the Swedish Migration Agency once the deadline for voluntary return had expired; this did not apply to adults living with their children. On 9 June 2016, the Council of the European Union decided to suspend the obligations of Sweden under the relocation decisions (EU) 2015/1523 and (EU) 2015/1601 until 16 June 2017.

Consequently, and despite Sweden not receiving any asylum seekers relocated from Italy or Greece in 2016, it continued its resettlement efforts, finalising the resettlement of the 491 individuals pledged in the framework of the Council decision. In November 2016, Sweden pledged to grant legal admission to 1,927 Syrian nationals who were present in Turkey and clearly required international protection. During 2016, Sweden resettled 1,907 persons in need of international protection within the framework of its national resettlement programme. The majority of persons were resettled from countries neighbouring Syria, as well as from the Horn of Africa and Central Africa/Great Lakes regions (EMN, 2016, p. 1). A salient point to make here regarding the numbers of young refugee newcomers to Sweden, Nelson reminds us that Sweden 'was tremendously successful' in integrating them, and in 2004 had absorbed 400 children a year. By 2011 this figure had grown to 2,600 but in 2015 '35,000 unaccompanied children claimed asylum in Sweden – most of whom had arrived in the last four months of 2015' (Nelson, 2016).

Certainly, the number and situation of unaccompanied minors are of particular interest from a Swedish perspective, as this type of immigration to Sweden is extensive compared to other European countries, in regard to both population size and in absolute terms. In 2013, the total number of unaccompanied minors seeking asylum in the EU's 28 countries was 12,730, according to Eurostat. Sweden received the largest group: 3,852 children. Germany (2,485), the United Kingdom (1,265) and Austria (935) were next (Çelikaksoy and Wadensjö, 2015b, p. 3). The following numbers were reported by Çelikaksoy and Wadensjö in their description of the development and demographic makeup of migrant unaccompanied minors to Sweden, and their educational and employment characteristics:

> Unaccompanied minors arriving in Sweden are generally refugees or in need of protection, and most of them who apply for a residence permit have their applications granted. Out of the 1,955 unaccompanied minors who were granted residence permits by the Swedish Migration Board (which is the first instance) in 2013, 8,384 were granted residence permits as Convention refugees, 1,093 as persons in need of protection, 465 due to particularly distressing circumstances, and 13 for other reasons. In the same year, 435 applications were rejected, an additional 166 were rejected with reference to the Dublin

Regulation, 9 and 386 people withdrew their application or left the country without formally withdrawing their application.

(Çelikaksoy and Wadensjö, 2015a, p. 5)

This population is considered to be vulnerable because they fled while being unaccompanied by parents or legal guardians. To get to Sweden, they endure traumatic experiences and challenges (Çelikaksoy and Wadensjö, n.d., p. 1; Derluyn and Vervliet, 2012). In Sweden, unaccompanied minors or separated children are defined as children under the age of 18 who are outside of their home country or country of origin. They arrived in Sweden unaccompanied by a parent or other legal guardian and this type of migratory flow, which has been increasing around the world, is now regarded as the most fragile. In the research by Çelikaksoy and Wadensjö (2015b, p. 10), most unaccompanied refugee children in Sweden are 16–17 years of age; boys on average are older than girls on arrival; and those aged 18 or 19 years arrived when they were below 18 but are still included in the population register in the year they became 18 or 19.

In Sweden unaccompanied minors arrive predominantly as asylum seekers and not via other channels and around 82 percent each year are granted a permanent residence permit. Responsibilities for looking after unaccompanied minors in Sweden changed on 1 July 2006, with local governments taking over from the Migration Board (Swedish Migration Agency, 2018). Also, the National Board of Health and Welfare is in charge of supervising the municipalities and developing guidance, recommendations and supervision for care. When a child enters Sweden he or she spends some time at an arrival centre following which a municipality covers the reception aspects (Çelikaksoy and Wadensjö, 2015a, p. 4). Specifically, the government issued the Reception for Settlement Act on 1 March 2016, which centralised the power for deciding how many recognised refugees as well as resettled would be assigned to a municipality which then had the responsibility to receive and organise accommodation for them (for four years). This decision was taken so that the responsibility to host throughout the country was spread out more evenly (OECD, 2018, p. 107). During the asylum-seeking process all unaccompanied minors obtain a temporary guardian. The child is able to have a permanent guardian if a permanent stay can in fact be granted in this situation. In municipalities the social services take care of living and daily care needs. All refugee children have the right to start school immediately following their arrival regardless of the stage of their asylum claim (Çelikaksoy and Wadensjö, 2015a, p. 4).

Overview of education in Sweden for refugee children

Asylum-seeking children have full access to Sweden's school system and they are to a great extent integrated in the country's regular schools. Although they are not covered by the law obliging children between the ages of 6 and 16 to attend school, they still have the right to attend. In Sweden, compulsory education ends at age 16, but pupils who are still enrolled in upper-secondary school when turning 17 or 18 have the right to continue their education like regular students, even in the case they do not have a recognised asylum-seeker status. Young adults arriving after the age of 18 can attend general adult education or Swedish for immigrants classes for adults to learn basic Swedish (Crul et al., 2016; Crul, 2017, p. 6). The general policy in Sweden is to keep children in international classes only for a very short period. Pupils are then transferred as quickly as possible to regular classes, often with additional courses in second-language education. Partly, this is enabled by the fact that Swedish schools offer second-language education as a regular subject from elementary school until the end of upper-secondary school, making it easier to incorporate students with a migration background – both refugees and others – into regular classes after a short period of time (Swedish Ministry of Education and Research, 2016).

Newcomers are entitled to the rights and measures that guarantee access to pre-primary, compulsory and vocational education, which targets their specific learning needs, provides lessons in their mother tongue and the necessary support required for intercultural education. Moreover, Sweden's municipalities and schools are responsible for ensuring newcomers obtain Swedish as a second language, and are expected to take initiatives to provide individualised support addressing specific needs to progress to an equivalent academic level as the Swedes (Rothschild, 2016). Swedish as a second language is offered in both elementary and upper-secondary school (up to the age of 18). It is the head teacher who decides which students will need to study Swedish as a second language (Rydin et al., 2012, p. 196). The fact that second-language education is also offered in upper-secondary schools is particularly important for refugee children who arrive aged 12 or older. Swedish as a second language is a subject with separate teaching materials (syllabus) and instructions, equal to teaching Swedish as a first language (Bourgonje, 2010, pp. 48 and 50). Specially trained teachers instruct Swedish as a second language (Nilsson and Bunar, 2016, p. 409).

Swedish Tuition for Immigrants is the most widely used programme that allows refugees and other immigrants to take language courses for free, in order to integrate more efficiently into society (Lindberg and Sandwall, 2007). Folkbergsskolan, a popular state school, is an example of measures taken by a Swedish institution that provides preparatory classes for newcomers in both Swedish and Arabic and demonstrates positive results in the simultaneous development of language and academic skills. Swedish from Day One is another example of a law that was introduced by Aida Hadzialic, a former refugee and current minister of secondary school, so that refugees have the opportunity to begin learning Swedish from the point of arrival, with the hope of enabling faster and more efficient interaction and integration into society.

The right to go to school is confirmed in law for those children still present in Sweden with an expulsion order and who have absconded with their parents (OECD, 2018, p. 36). Children between the ages of 16 and 19 often have to attend a preparatory course to improve their skills in Swedish and other core subjects before being able to access any form of vocational education. Once this preparatory phase is completed they are not prohibited in theory from undertaking a vocational course. If a teenager begins a three-year course at the age of 16 or 17 and is still in Sweden without a permit two years later, they can continue their course. However, persons who are over 18 on arrival in Sweden do not have access to secondary education (Joseph, 2015, p. 44). Children also have the right to lessons in their own mother tongue on a regular basis, if there are more than five pupils with the same language in the area. Itinerant mother-tongue teachers are employed for that purpose. Access to upper-secondary school education was curtailed following the introduction of the temporary law in 2016 (Skodo, 2018). Since amendments to the law that entered into force in June 2017, it is possible to obtain a residence permit allowing applicants to continue their studies. Many factors influence whether the person may get a residence permit for upper-secondary education studies. The rules are different for asylum seekers and for people with a temporary residence permit that they wish to extend. The rules also vary depending on whether the person is an unaccompanied child, whether he or she is studying on a national programme or on an induction programme, and in some cases on the date the first application for asylum was received (OECD, 2018; Skodo, 2018; Swedish Ministry of Education and Research, 2016).

The duration of the residence permit depends inter alia on the course's length and whether it is a national or induction programme. A residence permit can be granted for 4 years or 13 months. An applicant is also entitled to obtain a residence permit valid for 6 months after the course is completed. The amendment is not only applicable to unaccompanied children; young people arriving in Sweden together with their families may also apply for a residence permit on the grounds of their upper-secondary school studies, and this applies to people over the age of 18 but under 25. There have been criticisms pointing out that very few people match all criteria to be granted a residence permit on this ground. The government has proposed new legislation that will be presented to parliament, which will make it easier to be granted a residence permit to finish secondary education for those who turn 18 during the handling of their case at the Migration Agency or the relevant courts. This possibility will, as the draft proposal is now formulated, only exist for those unaccompanied children that registered their asylum application before 24 November 2015. The law was proposed to enter into force in July 2018 (Brendler-Lindqvist et al., 2014; Juárez et al., 2018; Karageorgiou, 2016).

Syrian refugee children in Sweden's education and employment systems

This section briefly looks at descriptions of education that have been experienced by Syrian refugee children. It investigates refugee practice in education for newly arrived children as well as refugee and asylum-seeking children in Swedish schools.

Sweden has been one of the largest receiving countries of unaccompanied minors over recent years, compared to other EU member states. This population is considered 'vulnerable' due to their young age during the fleeing process combined with the fact that they are unaccompanied by their parents or legal guardians (Derluyn and Vervliet, 2012). These children face heightened vulnerability due to exploitation, and violations of their rights by virtue of their age and status (CRC, 2016). The global movement of unaccompanied and separated children presents challenges for children's rights and well-being. Thus, research on unaccompanied minors has often focused on the vulnerabilities of this group, which reflects itself especially with regard to mental health (Derluyn and Broekaert, 2008). However, studies have increasingly stressed the strength, resilience and agency of unaccompanied minors, despite the traumatic experiences and challenges (Luster et al., 2010). The majority of analyses in this line of research focus on their situation and experiences during different stages of the migration, asylum, reception and introduction into the new destination country. Only a very few large-scale studies examined the refugees' situation in the labour market after they have received their permits to stay in the destination country. The question of how well-being should be defined still remains largely unresolved although there are common guidelines used in most definitions, such as agency (Dodge et al., 2012). Thus, the discourse on unaccompanied minors in relation to vulnerability versus resilience and agency is directly linked to the well-being of this group. Some of the aspects identified by Ryff (1989) that constitute well-being are autonomy, environmental mastery and realisation of potential, which boils down to the ability of directing one's work/life conditions by how one responds to challenges. As discussed earlier, unaccompanied minors are a group facing several challenges before, during and after the migration process. Thus, their situation in Sweden's labour market is an indicator of, among other factors, how they respond to the challenges of that particular destination country. From an immigration perspective, labour market incorporation can be seen as a key indicator of well-being, since it leads to access to money, possessions, networks, knowledge and practice on how the society and the labour market functions, as well as language proficiency. Subsequently, employment status can be an indicator of well-being in the labour market. Young workers, as with migrants and women, are particularly affected by precarious work situations, although to the best of our knowledge there are no studies on unaccompanied minors utilising large-scale data sets.

Insecure/precarious jobs in Sweden mean that for refugee children and young people, having suitable living conditions and foreseeable upward mobility and continued career paths cannot be predicted. This situation has recently been documented in-depth by one recent if undated study (for the following, see Pasquarello et al., n.d.) who generated important statistics on the employment of Syrian refugees in Sweden. Firstly, in terms of labour market integration, on completing introduction classes, many people face difficulties when entering the job market. Only 21.5 percent of males were employed within one year of completing the introduction programme organised by the Employment Service in 2015, and the rates were even lower (7.5 percent) for women, although 50 percent of all refugees find work after eight years in Sweden. Secondly, not only are the lower labour market integration levels consistent in other analyses, but a major hurdle for Syrian refugees is their lack of previous education and highly valued skillsets or qualifications. Migrants need a minimum of three years of post-secondary education in order to be successful in obtaining work. However, the effect of formal education on employment and earnings is especially positive if some education or labour market experience is achieved in Sweden. Thirdly, and interestingly, it is found that living in Stockholm when compared to other large Swedish cities, and being young (as well as well educated) does lead to a greater chance of being employed. Fourthly, for newcomers who are highly skilled, the Swedish government developed a 'fast track', the first of which was implemented in September 2015. These 'fast tracks' are organised by the Employment Service in cooperation with professional institutions and try to quickly integrate new arrivals with desirable skillsets into the workplace. Within six months of launching the first programme (which was for chefs), 21 other 'fast tracks' were developed for healthcare professionals, teachers and pre-school teachers.

Possible future challenges and recommendations

A major challenge now facing Swedish society inferred in this chapter is the problem of increasing residential segregation. Segregation affects all aspects of community life, ranging from economic and social relationships to the status, reputation and self-confidence of the population (Bell, 2007; Noreisch, 2007). Among the incoming refugee population in Sweden are troubling signs and symptoms of gangs and organised criminal networks gaining ground among first- and second-generation immigrant youth in socially deprived areas (Bunar, 2017, p. 13). For the destructive effects of segregation on vulnerable communities to be overcome, it is vital for the national and local governments and representatives of the local population, organisations and businesses to work together so that Syrian refugee children are well served by properly considered housing, social, labour market and education policies, combined with voices articulating local needs and properly implemented measures by local administrators, with the capacity to provide palpable alternatives.

Research on Syrian refugees in other countries has demonstrated the importance of how education policy for refugees must incorporate three interrelated domains – school and home/community environments in the development of quality education for learners. For example, Madziva and Thondhlana (2017) focus on a group of Syrian refugees who arrived in the United Kingdom in December 2015, developing a model (with the English language playing a critical role) emphasising not only the importance of these intersecting environments, but also the inputs/processes that are crucial to achieving quality education for refugees.

This is the sort of strategy required to overcome the Syrian refugees' manifestation of several mental health issues, and was noted by Tinghög (2017) who analysed the prevalence of anxiety, post-traumatic stress disorder, depression, low subjective well-being and post-migration stress among 1,215 randomly selected Syrian refugees in Sweden. A majority fulfilled the criteria of at least one of the studied types of mental ill health and almost 75 percent met multiple criteria. Depression emerged as the most common type (40.2 percent), followed by low subjective well-being (37.7 percent), anxiety 31.8 percent and post-traumatic stress disorder (29.9 percent). Forced separation from family or close friends was estimated to have been experienced by 67.9 percent, while torture was estimated to 31.0 percent. It was calculated that 19.8 percent had often felt excluded in Swedish society and 50.2 percent had often felt sad because of not being reunited with family members. This is an important challenge to overcome but also Sweden's education authorities should understand it is a challenge to continue what is already working. In one account published in early 2018, Abrams (2018) told the story of Noor, a young Syrian refugee student who did well compared to Ammar who ended up in the United Kingdom. Noor – who in his previous life was a child tailor – within a month of his arrival in Sweden was put into a foster family and in school, whereas Ammar struggled for months to find a school in Nottingham and then was only offered basic courses that did not meet his needs. Arriving in Malmö, Noor was taken to the Välkomsten or the 'Welcoming', the first port of call for new arrivals in Sweden. He was then quickly assigned a town, Helsingborg, a foster family and a school place at Nicolaiskolan, one of five schools in the town that are designated to take these young people. Noor started a business making sustainable fabric shopping bags and struggling to fulfil clients' demands. On the other hand, Ammar was ignored by his local council in Nottingham, waited six months and when offered a college place it was to study subjects that had nothing to do with his desire to do medicine: English, maths and ICT.

School segregation and an increasing achievement gap is another current and future challenge that desperately needs to be addressed. School segregation emerges partly because of the attendance zone principle for allocation of students between schools. Thus, students from a particular neighbourhood are admitted to their nearest public school. Many newly arrived students are ending up in immigrant-dominated schools in socially deprived neighbourhoods in large cities or in one single school in smaller municipalities. It is this tendency that partly contributes to increased segregation, and partly Syrian refugee children suffer most from its effects. For example, in the last few years Syrian refugee children have developed what the Swedish call *uppgivenhetssyndrom*, a syndrome in which they have given up on life due to the pressures of having to seek asylum after a traumatic migration, and do their education in very unfamiliar surroundings (Brink, 2017).

In the last four years, approximately 48,000 unaccompanied minors have applied for asylum in Sweden, and the majority of them are 15–17-year-old boys, mainly from Afghanistan, Iraq, Somalia, Syria, Morocco and Eritrea. Many of those unaccompanied children who arrived in earlier years did manage to find their places in the labour market (Çelikaksoy and Wadensjö, 2015b), proving their resilience and ambition (Bunar, 2017, p. 13). However, there are only very few unaccompanied minors who graduate from a national upper-secondary programme (Denkelaar, 2018, pp. 9–10). There are also worrying signs that some unaccompanied young boys are getting involved in petty crimes (Bunar, 2017, p. 13). It is a challenge, but an imperative one that must be resolved, for social service providers (i.e. schools, social services, police, legal guardians and school counsellors) to ensure that Syrian refugee children's education and social needs are properly responded to. It is of the upmost importance to find alternative educational paths, especially for those who drop out of the Language Introduction Program.

What, then, are the recommendations that can be made to improve the education and outcomes for Syrian refugee children in Sweden? Syrian refugee children experience many traumatic events, which have placed them at great risk of mental health issues like post-traumatic stress disorder, depression and psychosomatic injuries. These are conditions that have serious implications for the children's long-term social, cognitive and education development. It is evident that many fall behind significantly in their schooling or drop out altogether. To help families navigate the resettlement process in Sweden, policy makers and practitioners can conduct a number of steps to ensure Syrian children can access high-quality, tailored and *consistent* education with the attendant mental healthcare facilities. The initial recommendation that comes to mind when examining the Swedish context is to ensure that, irrespective of their migration status, legal barriers that prevent or impede access to education are removed. This is especially important for unaccompanied asylum seekers aged 18 and older.

There are several recommendations that need to be made in order to mitigate the current situation in Sweden where educational segregation is evident. It is important that Syrian refugee children do not have separate classes for an extended period of time, nor should they be part of schools only for newcomers. The following recommendations are suggested, given that education-related recommendations cannot operate in a vacuum, but only when schools work together with local communities and civic societies so that both Syrian refugee children and their parents are well integrated into local Swedish networks:

- Helping students learn the destination country's language will support them to retain their first language.
- Training educators to recognise the signs of trauma and develop the skills to help children cope with their trauma or loss.
- Working with families and individuals to address trauma and mental health problems, and drawing on the support from Syrian professionals – if and where possible – to ensure culturally appropriate treatment.

- Offering more teachers with training and qualifications in Swedish as a second language; there is furthermore an urgent need to organise shorter courses for all teaching staff on the structure and pedagogical content of learning Swedish as a second language.
- Providing multifaceted, culturally sensitive services in school contexts, backed up with access to health centres, community centres and traditional therapy offices.
- Introducing awareness education for non-immigrant parents to circumvent stigmatisation and fears of integration measures influencing their children negatively.
- While appropriate diagnostic tests, based on scientifically produced and tested material, are currently available on students' previous school background, knowledge and experiences, it is apparent that the testing process lacks individualisation, results are not always communicated to all concerned teachers and they are rarely used at upper-secondary schools.
- Ensuring there is a well-planned transfer from introductory to regular classes, and continuous bilingual and social scaffolding in regular classes, to promote optimal learning.

In a comment on the system in the United Kingdom regarding the education of refugee children, McIntyre (2017) recommends the Swedish way of schooling whereby refugee students and their families can access two hours of Swedish-language tuition as part of their residence permit. The reality is that with regard to language learning, a bilingual environment is the most successful. It means that a child's first language is continued and this enables them to learn a second or third language more quickly. Young refugees are therefore more likely to complete their education in their new country – becoming full members of their 'post-settlement' society.

Conclusion

The Swedish asylum system – which had long been one of the world's most efficient and generous – experienced an unprecedented challenge towards the end of 2015. As the number of refugees and migrants arriving in Sweden surged, processing times for asylum applications grew and emergency housing reached virtually full capacity. Consequently, in the education system schools struggled to enrol and teach young refugee children, who made up nearly half of asylum applicants in 2015. The pace of arrivals along with the existing housing, teacher and interpreter shortages meant that this robust system had now reached a crisis point. Swedish policy makers responded to these pressures in two main ways. Firstly, they introduced measures aimed at reducing future arrivals, including checkpoints at the border with Denmark and, controversially, lowering the level of benefits and rights offered to protection beneficiaries. The second and longer-term response has been to invest heavily in integration.

Looking ahead, the full outcomes of the migration and asylum crisis in Sweden are yet to be determined. With a system that is predicated on the long-term acceptance of refugee people into the country, what is critical here is the successful integration of Syrian refugee families. Syrian children's education in Sweden has in many ways been influenced by the legal and regulatory changes that were established in 2015–16. Their integration into Swedish society will be ultimately undermined if refugees' rights are reduced. Overall, one gets the sense that in Sweden the local implementation with respect to education opportunities for refugee and asylum-seeking children is in line with the legal frameworks. The fact that children are entitled to tuition in their mother tongue is regarded as very positive. However, a number of problems remain with respect to mother-tongue tuition, teaching Swedish as a second language, study guidance and teacher support. What is now very troubling in Sweden and requiring serious attention are the education rights of 'hidden' or undocumented children. According to the UN Committee of the Rights of the Child, Sweden – despite its reputation for human rights and a fairly liberal disposition to other social/ethnic groups in its borders – cannot guarantee the right to education for these children.

References

Abrams, Fran (2018). 'In Sweden, Noor Went Straight to School; in Britain, Ammar Waited Six Months'. *Guardian*, 13 February. Retrieved 18 November 2018 from www.theguardian.com/education/2018/feb/13/sweden-school-britain-education-young-refugees.

BBC News (2016). 'EU Migrant Crisis: Sweden May Reject 80,000 Asylum Claims'. 28 January. Retrieved 15 November 2018 from www.bbc.com/news/world-europe-35425735.

Bell, C. (2007). 'Space and Place: Urban Parents' Geographical Preferences for Schools'. *Urban Review*, 39, 375–404.

Berg, Kasja (2016). 'Why the Swedish Make a U-Turn on Refugees: Expel up to 80,000 Asylum Seekers'. *Globalo: News behind the News*, 19 February. Retrieved 26 October from www.globalo.com/why-the-swedish-make-a-u-turn-on-refugees/.

Bourgonje, P. (2010). 'Education for Refugee and Asylum Seeking Children in OECD Countries: Case Studies from Australia, Spain, Sweden and the United Kingdom'. Brussels: Education International.

Brendler-Lindqvist, M., Norredam, M. and Hjern, AndersHjern (2014). 'Duration of Residence and Psychotropic Drug Use in Recently Settled Refugees in Sweden: A Register-Based Study'. *International Journal for Equity in Health*, 13, 122.

Brink, Susan (2017). 'In Sweden, Hundreds of Refugee Children Gave Up on Life'. *Goats and Soda: Stories of Life in a Changing World*, 30 March. Retrieved 18 November 2018 from www.npr.org/sections/goatsandsoda/2017/03/30/521958505/only-in-sweden-hundreds-of-refugee-children-gave-up-on-life.

Bunar, Nihad (2017). *Migration and Education in Sweden: Integration of Migrants in the Swedish School Education and Higher Education Systems NESET II ad hoc Question No. 3/2017*. Stockholm: Stockholm University.

Çelikaksoy, Aycan and Wadensjö, Eskil (2015a). *Unaccompanied Minors and Separated Refugee Children in Sweden: An Outlook on Demography, Education and Employment*. IZA Discussion Paper No. 8963. Bonn.
Çelikaksoy, Aycan and Wadensjö, Eskil (2015b). *Unaccompanied and Separated Refugee Minors in Sweden*. Stockholm University Swedish Institute for Social Research and Stockholm University Linnaeus Center for Integration Studies.
Çelikaksoy, Aycan and Wadensjö, Eskil (n.d.). 'Unaccompanied Refugee Minors in Sweden: Education and Wellbeing in the Labor Market'. Retrieved 16 November 2018 from www.oru.se/globalassets/oru-sv/institutioner/hh/seminarieserien-nek/seminarie serie-nek—eskil-wadensjo-180412.pdf.
CRC (2016). 'Report of the 2016 Day of General Discussion: Children's Rights and Environment'. Geneva: Office of the High Commissioner on Human Rights.
Crouch, David (2015). 'Sweden Slams Shut Its Open-Door Policy towards Refugees'. *Guardian*, 24 November. Retrieved 15 November from www.theguardian.com/world/2015/nov/24/sweden-asylum-seekers-refugees-policy-reversal.
Crul, Maurice (2017). *Refugee Children in Education in Europe: How to Prevent a Lost Generation?* SIRIUS Network Policy Brief Series, Issue No. 7. Retrieved 26 October 2018 from www.sirius-migrationeducation.org/wp-content/uploads/2012/06/Refugee-children-in-education-in-Europe.-How-to-prevent-a-lost-generation.pdf.
Crul, Maurice (n.d.). 'Children of Immigrants and Refugees in Europe: Combining Outcomes of PISA Results and Results of Other International Surveys'. Retrieved 26 October 2018 from www.oecd.org/education/school/Maurice-Crul-RD11.pdf.
Crul, Maurice, Keskiner, Elif, Schneider, Jens, Lelie, Frans and Ghaeminia, Safoura (2016). 'No Lost Generation? Education for Refugee Children: A Comparison between Sweden, Germany, the Netherlands and Turkey'. Retrieved 26 October 2018 from http://hmm.igeucla.org/wp-content/uploads/2017/01/Education-for-refugee-children-Crul-et-al-DRAFT.pdf.
Denkelaar, Monique (2018). *Multi-Country Partnership to Enhance the Education of Refugee and Asylum-Seeking Youth in Europe – PERAE: Refugee Education in Sweden*. Stockholm: SIRIUS: Policy Network on Migrant Education.
Derluyn, I. and Broekaert, E. (2008). 'Unaccompanied Refugee Children and Adolescents: The Glaring Contrast between a Legal and a Psychological Perspective'. *International Journal of Law and Psychiatry*, 31(4), 319–330.
Derluyn, I. and Vervliet, M. (2012). 'The Wellbeing of Unaccompanied Refugee Minors'. In D. Ingleby, A. Krasnik, V. Lorant, and O. Razum (eds), *Health Inequalities and Risk Factors among Migrants and Ethnic Minorities*, Vol. 1. Antwerpen/Apeldoorn: Garant, pp. 95–109.
Dodge, R., Daly, A., Huyton, J. and Sanders, L. (2012). 'The Challenge of Defining Wellbeing'. *International Journal of Wellbeing*, 2(3), 222–235. doi: doi:10.5502/ijw.v2i3.4.
EMN (European Migration Network) (2016). *Country Factsheet: Sweden 2016*. European Commission.
Faughey, Deirdre (2015). 'Government Funding and Refugee Migration in Nordic Region'. *International Education News*, 30 September. Retrieved 26 October 2018 from https://internationalednews.com/tag/sweden/.
Fratzke, Susan (2017). *Weathering Crisis, Forging Ahead: Swedish Asylum and Integration Policy*. Transatlantic Council on Migration/Migration Policy Institute. Retrieved 16 November 2018 from file:///C:/Users/public.DESKTOP-4QOFEQF/Downloads/TCM-Asylum-Sweden-FINAL.pdf.

Johnson, Simon and Sennero, Johan (2015). 'Sweden Budgets Extra $3 Billion for Jobs, Education, Refugee Influx'. *Reuters*, 21 September. Retrieved 16 November 2018 from www.reuters.com/article/us-sweden-government/sweden-budgets-extra-3-billion-for-jobs-education-refugee-influx-idUSKCN0RL0F420150921?utm_content=buffer8529d&utm_medium=social&utm_source=twitter.com&utm_campaign=buffer.

Joseph, George (2015). *Aida. Asylum Information Database. Country Report: Sweden*. European Council on Refugees and Exiles.

Juárez, S.P., Drefahl, S., Dunlavy, A. and Rostial, M. (2018). 'All-Cause Mortality, Age at Arrival, and Duration of Residence among Adult Migrants in Sweden: A Population-Based Longitudinal Study'. *SSM-Population Health*, 6, 16–25.

Karageorgiou, Eleni (2016). 'Downgrading Asylum Standards to Coerce Solidarity: Sweden as a Case in Point'. *EU Immigration and Asylum Law and Policy*, 13 May. Retrieved 25 February 2019 from http://eumigrationlawblog.eu/downgrading-asylum-standards-to-coerce-solidarity-sweden-as-a-case-in-point/.

Lindberg, Inger and Sandwall, Karin (2007). 'Nobody's Darling? Swedish for Adult Immigrants: A Critical Perspective'. *Prospect*, 22(3), 79–95.

Luster, T., Qin, D., Bates, L., Rana, M. and Lee, J. (2010). 'Successful Adaption among Sudanese Unaccompanied Minors: Perspectives of Youth and Foster Parents'. *Childhood*, 17(2), 197–211.

Madziva, Roda and Thondhlana, Juliet (2017). 'Provision of Quality Education in the Context of Syrian Refugee Children in the UK: Opportunities and Challenges'. *Compare: A Journal of Comparative and International Education*, 47(6), 942–961.

Mahmoud, Ghalib M. (2016). 'Employment Challenges Affecting the Recent Influx of Refugees in the European Union'. Law School Student Scholarship. Paper 826. Retrieved 26 October 2018 from https://scholarship.shu.edu/cgi/viewcontent.cgi?referer=https:// www.google.com.au/&httpsredir=1&article=1834&context=student_scholarship.

Mangrio, Elisabeth, Zdravkovic, Slobodan and Carlson, Elisabeth (2018). 'A Qualitative Study of Refugee Families' Experiences of the Escape and Travel from Syria to Sweden'. *BMC Research Notes*, 11, 594. doi: doi:10.1186/s13104–13018–3702–3701.

McIntyre, Joanna (2017). 'Refugees Welcome? How UK and Sweden Compare on Education for Young Migrants'. *Conversation*, 1 June. Retrieved 18 November 2018 from http://theconversation.com/refugees-welcome-how-uk-and-sweden-compare-on-education-for-young-migrants-74939.

Nelson, Fraser (2016). 'Sweden Is a Perfect Example of How Not to Handle the Great Migration'. *Telegraph*, 28 January. Retrieved 16 November 2018 from www.telegraph.co.uk/news/worldnews/europe/sweden/12128598/Sweden-is-a-perfect-example-of-how-not-to-handle-the-Great-Migration.html.

Nilsson, J. and Bunar, N. (2016). 'Educational Responses to Newly Arrived Students in Sweden: Understanding the Structure and Influence of Post-Migration Ecology'. *Scandinavian Journal of Educational Research*, 60(4), 399–416.

Noreisch, K. (2007). 'Choice as Rule, Exception and Coincidence: Parents' Understandings of Catchment Areas in Berlin'. *Urban Studies*, 44, 1307–1328.

OECD (2018). *Working Together for Local Integration of Migrants and Refugees*. Paris: OECD Publishing.

Ostrand, N. (2015). 'The Syrian Refugee Crisis: A Comparison of Responses by Germany, Sweden, the United Kingdom, and the United States'. *Journal on Migration and Human Security*, 3(3), 255–279.

Pasquarello, J., Bevelander, P., Törngren, P.B., Emilsson, H. and Irastorza, N. (n.d.). 'Sweden's Response to Syrian-Conflict Refugee Settlement'. University Technology Sydney. Retrieved 26 February 2019 from www.uts.edu.au/research-and-teaching/our-research/centre-business-and-social-innovation/research/projects-0.

Rothschild, Nathalie (2016). 'On the Frontline of Integration: How Swedish Schools Are Helping Refugees'. *Guardian*, 26 June. Retrieved 5 January 2019 from www.theguardian.com/teachernetwork/2016/jun/26/on-the-frontline-of-integration-how-swedish-schools-are-helpingrefugees.

Rydin, I., Eklund, M., Högdin, S. and Sjöberg, U. (2012). 'Country Report Sweden'. In A. Nonchev and N. Tagarov (eds), *Integrating Refugee and Asylum-Seeking Children in the Educational Systems of EU Member States*. Sofia: CSD.

Ryff, C.D. (1989). 'Happiness Is Everything, or Is It? Explorations on the Meaning of Psychological Well-Being'. *Journal of Personality and Social Psychology*, 57(6), 1069–1081.

sa/ks (2015). 'How Many Refugee Children Can Sweden Take?' *IRIN: The Inside Story on Emergencies*, 15 October. Retrieved 15 November 2018 from www.irinnews.org/analysis/2015/10/15.

Skodo, Admir (2018). *Sweden: By Turns Welcoming and Restrictive in Its Immigration Policy*. Migration Policy Institute, 6 December. Retrieved 3 January 2019 from www.migrationpolicy.org/article/sweden-turns-welcoming-and-restrictive-its-immigration-policy.

Swedish Migration Agency (2018). 'Migrationsverket'. Retrieved 3 January 2019 from www.migrationsverket.se/English/About-the-Migration-Agency/Migration-to-Sweden/History.html.

Swedish Ministry of Education and Research (2016). *OECD Review of Policies to Improve the Effectiveness of Resource Use in Schools (School Resources Review). Country Background Report: Sweden*. Report No. U2014/3484/S.

Tinghög, P. (2017). 'Mental Ill-Health, Trauma and Adverse Post-Migratory Experiences among Refugees from Syria in Sweden'. *European Journal of Public Health*, 27, Supplement 3. Retrieved 3 May 2019 from https://doi.org/10.1093/eurpub/ckx187.126.

6

DISCUSSION AND COMPARISON OF REFUGEE CHILDREN IN EDUCATION IN AUSTRALIA AND SWEDEN

The present-day situation regarding the refugee crisis that became a globally serious one, and the politics surrounding it and how refugee children should be cared for and educated, has now exceeded any initial forcible displacement caused by war. Serious implications regarding how displaced children and their families are impacted need to be addressed, as indeed the previous chapters on Sweden and Australia have shown. However, it is very important to remember that these people did not choose to leave their homeland. They have in fact been forced to evacuate in desperate circumstances and seek safety and security in a new country. Chapters 4 and 5 examined the contexts and resettlement policies and opportunities available for education to support and protect people who found refuge in Sweden and Australia. It was evident in these countries' sometimes quite different government policies and expectations of the wider societies around them that education and schools now play a major role in the settlement and assimilation of refugees and their children, especially where the objective is to improve their physical, mental health and well-being, and ensure they can fit as much as possible into the society that has accepted them.

This chapter reports and discusses the school experiences of refugee students living in Australia and in Sweden by way of making a comparative analysis, buttressed by the author's previous analysis of conditions for refugees in Lebanon during her study in that country in 2017/18. Comparisons are also made with what other researchers found on the topic of refugee children's experiences in Australia, Sweden and Lebanon. A variety of different factors that affect and influence the educational opportunities for refugee children on many levels within their educational institution are explained here. Our aim is to hear, describe and elucidate the voices of the refugee students about firstly, what happens in their classes? Secondly, how do they feel about their teachers and subject areas? Thirdly, how do they find second-language learning? Fourthly, what do they think of their current situations? Fifthly, what support does the school provide for them with i.e. counselling, access to psychologists, extra tuition, etc.? And finally, what do they think of their host country?

Classroom description

This question was truly intriguing as most refugee students described their classrooms as being warm, bright and happy. It was noticeable whenever this question was raised that almost the same smile was received from all. In the context of Australian classrooms, it was commented by Alia 'it seems that teachers put so much effort to make the room look happy'. Another student Mohsin added that 'they are not just happy, there is something about the classroom that makes you feel safe', further stating 'it scares me to think of it this way … hmm … I don't know, the classes are not just lovely, but too lovely.' Najmeh said 'Our classroom is fine. We have facilities and resources. The classroom itself is very comfortable and warm. There are computers and modern equipment for all to share comfortably.'

The above-mentioned students' comments were echoed by refugees attending classes in Sweden. For example, when we asked Mouna to describe her classroom, she could not sit still in her seat but started pointing to the plain wall in the interview room. While walking towards it she would say,

> On this wall we will have all these beautiful and colourful photos of happy faces of all of us, and on the other wall we can see our art work that we have created ourselves and the third wall is also decorated with more things that the teacher put up that she wants us to see all the time, it is just nice.

Another child, Samira, remarked that 'the room always looks clean and tidy and that makes me happy and reminds me of how mama used to keep the house in Syria before we left'. Meanwhile Hassan used the following description, 'I think that teachers like to see happy things when they come to teach so they keep their classrooms always clean and pretty'. Compared to these responses, the answers received from refugee students in various make-shift schools situated in Lebanon were not as moving, especially since a few of them described their classrooms as akin to a sardine can, and being crowded with students on top of each other. Others said that they hated having to attend the afternoon shift allocated to them by the relevant government department because it made them feel like a rejected group who had simply received the 'left-overs'.

Student–teacher relationship

War has a demoralising influence on people. It does not only impact on losses of lives, possessions and other belongings; it also leaves individuals physically, psychologically or emotionally scarred or damaged and influences their future lives and outlook on the world around them. According to one study by the World Bank, one vitally important factor is education because it is the key institution that can influence the development of many characteristics such as skills, values, behaviours, attitudes and help build resilience (World Bank, 2013). The important point is made here that helping refugees depends on closer collaboration between disaster risk-management communities, dealing for example with climate-related issues, by incorporation of climate and disaster resilience into broader community-development processes. These characteristics spark new hopes in the lives of individuals who have experienced trauma and loss and it is important to note that the theme of people having a sense of resilience should not be underestimated. Despite the fact that many people from war-torn countries encounter, witness and survive trauma, not all develop significant mental disorders (Rosner et al., 2003), one researcher notes that refugee people reveal enormous 'courage and strength by coping with conditions of extreme deprivation and surviving against adversity' (Tiong, 2006, p. 8). Once refugee status has been established, a person has to learn to master the demands of resettlement in a foreign country, and equally importantly, the loss and separation from their family and culture (Schweitzer et al., 2006, 2007; Fernando and Ferrari, 2011). Despite this turmoil, research evidence suggests many refugee people do go on to thrive and prosper in their new country and surroundings. However, it is noticeable that professionals continue to employ a Western medical model that automatically places refugees' experiences of hardship, deprivation and distress in the terrain of psychopathology, rather than simply accepting it as a 'normal' response to an abnormal situation (Tufan et al., 2012). Consequently, refugees' sense of resilience is often obscured by the pervasiveness of the trauma narrative in refugee people's lives (Papadopoulos, 2001). Given that definitions of resilience will differ, it is often associated with a person's ability to bounce back and, as Wagnild and Collins (2009, p. 1) assert, 'following adversity and challenge connotes inner strength, competence, optimism, flexibility and the ability to cope effectively when faced with adversity'.

Teachers' attitudes and dedication can often make or break students' enthusiasm for learning. When the school children were asked about the teachers/teaching approach in schools that they went to, many positive answers were received, demonstrating their satisfaction with teachers' kindness and attitudes. A few insisted that their teachers treat them like they were their own children. The majority of refugee students who were interviewed in Australia and Sweden talked about their teachers and described them as being caring, welcoming and compassionate. For example, Mohsin said that his teachers in Australia are mostly very generous with their time and offer him help when he does not understand, and he added that all teachers tend to speak very fast and sometimes students cannot keep up with what is being stated. Mahmood thinks that Swedish people are the kindest at heart especially his teachers; and these thoughts were reflected in his statement when he said, 'Teachers have very kind hearts but always telling us what to do, not in an encouraging way but in a bossy way. I think that they don't have a good way of communicating their feelings with us and sometimes we misunderstand what their intentions are.' Refugee students observed how busy their teachers in schools in both Australia and Sweden are and they have made a few similar statements that reflect their perceptions, for example: 'teachers don't have time to correct our homework'; and 'the work we get given never gets checked', according to Alia, Mohsin and Ellie. In Lebanon on the other hand, most responses replicated voices of refugee students who seem to be experiencing hurt and neglect, for example when you hear Hakeem's comments that teachers have been telling them that they were not welcome because they burdened the schools and teachers have been expected to do extra work. This is echoed in recent work undertaken by Hall and Summers (2018), who commented on the pressure that Syrian refugee children experience.

Second-language learning

Australia and Sweden appear to have quite unique cases and policies in place when it comes to the development of their respective education sector. The cases that they deal with may in some ways be unique but ultimately they are overwhelming, particularly when considering that in other countries such as Lebanon, most of the refugees are from Iraq, Palestine and Syria and they all share the Arabic language. Many of the children who were interviewed for this study shared with us their experiences of their journey prior to arriving in their host country. Some of them remarked that they had stopped in one, two and in some cases three or more countries before reaching their final destination, be it Australia or Sweden (Spinks, 2013). In fact, one recent study by Tucker (2018) found a very high degree of destination specificity for Sweden for nearly all of the interviewed participants, but he followed an assessment based on people's desire to reach the country after comparing it to other European or Arab states. Most of the refugees had conducted prior research, drawing on information from social networks and other sources, in order to establish which European country would most easily and quickly give them opportunities such as language learning, work, education and citizenship.

It is evident that refugees have experienced different situations and overcome various circumstances along their journey; not all of them were lucky enough to have attended educational institutions that were available for them while waiting to go further abroad. As stated in the chapter on Australia, education is compulsory for all children until they turn 16 years of age or when they reach Year 10 in high school. Once they reach that age it will become their responsibility to decide what they would like to do: aim for higher education, follow a vocational pathway or start working somewhere. According to Zwi (2017) this is possible if the following conditions exist and are linked to that sense of resilience noted earlier: (1) being close to the family's own ethnic community; (2) knowing someone in Australia before immigrating and feeling supported by either their own ethnic group or the general community; and (3) the fact that Australians generally – but not always – display tolerance towards people of other cultures, nationalities and religions.

It is somewhat similar in Sweden where children have the option to opt for school once they turn 16; and those with a disability or from a poorer socio-economic environment are often encouraged to take the so called 'dual-system path' which is a form of company-based and school-complemented vocational training (Crul et al., 2017; Houghton, 2011). The law is not fully enforced in other countries such as Lebanon, for example, where the legal age for students to stay in schools is 15. Nevertheless, as recent commentaries (Attard, 2015; Anderson, 2016; Save the Children, 2018) have noted, many refugee children have been left out of school since their arrival in Lebanon, while those who attended temporarily and decided to leave school earlier than the required age are not followed or chased but left to wander as they please. To quote at length a publication by the organisation Save the Children in a context where there is very little motivation to learn a second language:

> Sometimes, families don't have enough to support their children, and they are forced to resort to cutting off education and sending their children to work, so child labor is the number one barrier. I know many children who can't go to school because they'd have to compromise their working hours. Families around here [at Mt Lebanon] tend to send their sons to work while enrolling their girls at school if they could. There was a girl at our Basic Literacy and Numeracy class who we referred to school. We were so happy that, after several years without education, she finally realised her dream. Unfortunately, two years after joining, she dropped out to get married. I think treatment [at public school] is a top issue. There is much violence at school … We've tried to solve this issue through our activities. We promoted integration, we told the children that we can't react with anger and that, instead, we should face up to the challenges and become better. Things have got a bit better in recent years. [At the Homework Support Group], we show respect and are putting them on the right track … But, as we often see, the shock happens with the transition, when they go to the formal school and find out it's not the same as here. Children are the future. They need to get back [to education] immediately. But when you have a generation deprived of education, the future is uncertain.
>
> (Save the Children, n.d., p. 22)

Australia and Sweden are nations where refugee children attend preparation or introductory classes for a year or two prior to transferring to the mainstream. When refugee students involved in this study were asked to describe some of the barriers they encountered, the main problem was language. It has proved to be a major challenge for Iraqi and Syrian refugees due to their original homeland curricula having been exclusively designed using the Arabic language. When we asked the refugee students in schools in Australia how they found the English language, we received many versions of one story leading to the same answer. The children's responses below provided us with some understanding of how they felt about learning a second language.

Firstly, Shadi was asked about his experience and he said, 'English is very difficult to learn and it makes me do really bad in school. I was very good at maths and science back home and now I struggle because most times I don't understand what my teacher is talking about.' Secondly, and on the other hand, Maysa referred to English as 'the language that keeps challenging me' and when asked her to explain what she meant she added: 'every time I think that I have mastered something another problem occurs ... I wish I have someone in school that can explain to me why certain things are the way they are and give me some examples related to the Arabic language so I can totally understand.' Another person, Ibrahim, who shied away when asked this question, eventually replied,

> I feel stupid not doing very well in many subjects because the language is so hard and so different. Can you imagine how difficult it can be if you had to even learn the alphabets? I hope that I can improve soon and not waste more of my life trying to get somewhere.

In Sweden, the same method and questions were practised and similar answers were shared again. Ellie is a 17 year old who claimed that he felt very frustrated having to learn to speak Swedish before he could do something with his life. He cursed the civil war raging in his home country and having to escape and leave his family to survive. Similarly, Hiba's words explained her frustration when she was trying to talk about her feelings in a language that she can hardly speak and she said, 'You lose half the meanings and the livelihood of your sentence while trying to make sense; it scares me to think that one day I will not remember who I once was.' Ihab begged me to speak more with him so he could hear the Arabic language and remember his native tongue which he greatly missed, while Alaa asked me to speak to his teachers and asked them to allow the refugees to speak Arabic with each other in school without being reprimanded. He remarked, 'They encourage us to speak Swedish to get better but they can't teach us well, it is boring and annoying the way they do it.' Najwa elicited the following comment with disappointment showing on her face, 'The language is all we have now and it hurts to speak to our Syrian friends in Swedish,' adding that 'It does not feel right.' These comments demonstrate that language is very important and is integral to the transmission of the children's culture and belonging. In fact, as the language was enjoyable and comfortable for them to speak, it facilitated communication between members of the same group (Smolicz and Secombe, 1981).

In this study, refugees speaking the Arabic language felt that their linguistic values associated them to a certain group and community. According to Smolicz (1979; Secombe and Zajda, 1999), humanistic sociology envisages a group's culture as made up of the cultural meanings or values which are shaped by members of a given group in various aspects of life, such as economics, religion, linguistics, family, friends, food, etc. The refugee children viewed the Arabic language as vital to their ongoing existence and to their sense of belonging to that culture. In their own words, Kareem and Ahmed both agreed that not being able to communicate in school with each other using their Arabic language made them feel strange to one another. Ahmed said with disappointment, 'I feel like an absolute idiot to talk to my best friend that I have known for years who lived few streets away from me in a language that I can barely speak or understand instead of our language.' Hassan suggested that learning another language is a bonus but it does not mean that they have forgotten their own. Mahmood confirmed what his peers said when he whispered,

> I would have loved to learn a language as a hobby, maybe to understand some TV shows or read some signs and to be able to speak to others but with the war forcing us to jump in situations like this it is not fun at all ... we feel as if we are trying to impress everyone around us and letting go of who we are.

The veracity of these comments are echoed in the study on Syrian and other refugee groups in Sweden by Wångdahl (2017), who documented the sheer difficulty in understanding another language in the health literacy context, not only in terms of being educated to speak and write in another language.

The situation in Lebanon varied slightly since the country's official language is Arabic while the curriculum is developed using either French or English to teach mathematics or science subjects in schools. The newly arrived refugees found the curriculum extremely difficult to master since the Ministry of Education insisted that the official teaching programme using the foreign language remains the same for all (MEHE, 2016). Therefore, many refugee children found schooling to be challenging and different to their previous experiences and many chose to avoid education completely. However, those who have enrolled in schools and started attending faced difficulties at the beginning while learning one of the languages used in their school and adjusting to the new way of school life. In Lebanon, the Ministry of Education implemented afternoon second-shift classes for Syrian refugees to segregate them from the Lebanese students, fearing that the quality of and desired outcomes of teaching would be seriously compromised (Lindberg Brekke, 2015 p. 77).

Another factor that has been brought to the author's attention during a five-year study (in collaboration with the Centre of Lebanese Studies and funded by the Spencer Foundation) is the importance that refugees place on their first language and hope to have educational opportunities. Doing so would allow them to maintain and improve Arabic reading and writing while learning the language of the host country in which they are currently living. Refugee students who attended schools or colleges where the Arabic language was being taught regularly indicated more enthusiasm for language learning during their interviews. Refugee children studying in Australian schools/colleges where Arabic was taught a few hours per week seemed happier and felt more confident learning English as a second language. They remarked that they used to get some examples translated during their Arabic classes to help them understand their subjects better. Najmeh said, 'My Arabic teacher was so nice and was always willing to make sense of some English lessons by teaching it to me in Arabic'; Ahmed also said that being at an Islamic college meant that his home language would always flourish and help him retain his parents' mother tongue and his cultural roots. The refugees in Sweden had a few hours of Arabic per week and, according to a few interviewees, these classes were the highlight of their day. Ihab was the first to say how much it meant to him having the opportunity to carry on with his Syrian home language while studying Swedish in Sweden. He was 'thrilled to have such luck', while Hannan also enjoyed the Arabic sessions that she took in school and said that they were very helpful for her because they helped her improve learning her second language. As mentioned in Chapter 5, McIntyre (2017) advocated and recommended that a bilingual environment is the most helpful for learning a second or third language successfully.

A large number of refugee children struggled with picking up a language and had been placed in classes that were for younger children; for example, some Year 9 students were put in Year 5 classrooms. This situation was not favoured by many refugees and a few interviews we conducted reflected this point. One student, Joumana, indicated that going to school was like starting from scratch; she said, 'I had to learn a language to study certain subjects which are compulsory anyway; this was not fair to us but there was no point complaining to anyone.' Mahdi noted that the school was harsh and teachers became exasperated with people not being able to speak the language of instruction for certain subjects. Last but not least, Mustafa, who is 15 years old remarked, 'I have been doing year nine for four years. I have done that in Syria twice and repeated it here and was told that I have to do it again. I have passed it three times but repeating it to improve my language.' It emphasises the point made by Shuayb et al. (2014, p. 100) in their study on refugee children's education in Lebanon that:

> The dearth of expertise in emergency education in schools was not only restricted to the classroom, but similarly affected admission policies. Traditionally, school placement tests for Lebanese children often included English, Arabic, and math tests. Yet the majority of the interviewed Syrian children were only given a single test in English, since this was viewed as the most significant barrier for their learning. On that basis, many students were demoted or had to repeat classes without the additional support to help them succeed.

As we can see from the above statements, refugee children commented on the difficulty of learning another language whether it be English in Australia, Swedish in Sweden or even French and English in Lebanon. They expressed their concerns and feelings about falling behind due to the struggle to keep up with the language, sometimes requesting help using their mother-tongue language. This was not only to provide support and boost their confidence in learning the second language, but also make them feel accepted for who they are, preserve their cultural values and to retain their identity.

Personal stories and current situations

As the title of this section states, personal stories were shared with the interviewers, bringing to light hidden and scared distant voices tinted with pain, suffering, heartache and trauma. When refugee students in Australia and Sweden were asked to share their experiences of having to leave their homes in Syria or Iraq during the civil war and reflect on some of the things that had happened on their journey to their country of destination, they were actually very surprised by this question as they weren't used to being asked it. When, for example, Aiya did her schooling in Australia she said that in class she is often told to let go of the past and focus on tomorrow, which is actually very difficult to do, and this sort of comment compounds people's ignorance of what war does to people. To emphasise this point, another student, Nagee, said that his teacher tells them in class that if they want to start learning fast and moving forward they cannot keep reflecting on what happened in their home country or in the refugee camps. Carol Barriuso, who recently worked as part of an EU initiative on education, youth and sport, in the capacity of the group's moderator, echoed this problem when asked about the challenges that teachers or schools encountered when integrating refugee children (eTwinning, 2017):

> international studies of refugee children and young people in exile indicate a high number of emotional and behavioural difficulties, primarily related to post-traumatic stress disorder (PTSD), sleeping problems, anxiety and depression. Many have experienced life threatening events and physical abuse prior to and during their flight, and suffer from the loss of parents, family and friends. So, the realities of the Newly Arrived Migrants can be very challenging and we should not forget their past when thinking about their integration in our schools. But education is not just about learning, it is about arriving, it is about taking in these kids and providing them a safe environment where to develop as a person.

With regard to Sweden, Kareem said, 'It is unusual you ask me that because all the time here teachers ask mostly about our future but not our past. Things like what do you want to do in the future? What are your plans? Where do you want to go? Nothing like your question.' It is evident that these students have felt some form of neglect by not being asked to share their experiences and to reinforce this perception, Maya in Sweden stated that she was told to 'stop depressing herself talking about the past and instead start planning her future'. Her future is very much attached to her past, as is her focus on learning the Swedish language properly and starting work. She wants her sister to live with her and not with the host family in another town which is two hours away. Furthermore, she would like to bring her mother to Sweden from Syria one day.

The majority of refugee students shared some unbelievable journeys and experiences with us, things they have seen, families they have left behind, memories that still haunt their sleep and wake them up at night. In Sweden, Hamzeh said that his journey was virtually a triathlon because he walked, swam and found a bike in Greece that he rode for a while during his trek to Sweden; he carried on naming the places he went through and said, 'We paid 3,500 Euros and sat on a tiny deflated boat from Turkey to Greece and went on foot to Macedonia, then Serbia where we traveled on donkeys' backs, Hungary, and we flew to Austria before getting into Stockholm.' Maya said that 'in Greece, they threw gas bombs at us'. One of them had suffered being imprisoned by the militant Islamist group Daesh which held him hostage for more than a year. A few other children said they went to Lebanon before being accepted to come to Australia while two families had been on a boat from Indonesia to Australia. They ended up in the Nauru detention centre for ten months after living in Kuwait for a short period of time, with stints in Turkey and Egypt before arriving at their country of destination. Kareem stated,

> I went with mum [and] they caught us and we had to go back to Turkey. Then we got on another boat and the sea guards caught us once again. We went on another boat which had over one hundred and eighty people jammed on top of each other like cattle. We were in the water for ten hours and waited for over eleven hours and started leaking and sinking, my parents need to get out of Syria and join us here soon.

What was most important for the majority of refugee students living in Sweden was learning the basic language so that they could find work. Essentially, they wanted to be together with their siblings, and it should be noted that very few who had their parents with them during their interviews talked about studying and going to university. For language-training intervention to work in Sweden for Syrian refugees, one research study documents evidence that a combination of mentorship and job-seeking resources improves the probability of finding employment. For instance, an assessment of Sweden's Introduction Programme concluded that adding an 'intensive coaching' dimension to existing language and employment preparation courses increases the chances of employment probability (Fanjul et al., 2018, p. 6).

In Australia, similar thoughts were shared about seeking employment sooner rather than later and very few mentioned marriage when they spoke about their future plans. Ayia said, 'I am thinking about taking a hairdressing course as soon as I do the English lessons. I need to work but no one will give me a job unless I have the language.' Similarly, Najmeh spoke about the unlimited opportunities that she had ahead of her in Australia and said, 'Thank God I don't have to get married like my cousin Zahra who lives in Jordan and had to marry this much older man who promised to look after her and her family.' Najmeh spoke with confidence about finding a good job in the future, one that will make her and her parents proud. Not only girls were happy about having the options of finding work once they managed the language but boys like Ibrahim also seemed keen to start work once studying English was completed; Ibrahim wanted to support his family who worked tirelessly to get all four children somewhere safe. Meanwhile in Lebanon, it was a totally different scenario, where the majority of Syrian refugee students talked about finding work suitable for them and allowing them to support their families with a large number of girls saying they would find the right person and get married when they reached 15 or 16 years of age. 'It is not easy to avoid marriage when you know that it is the only hope for you to be able to survive and lessen the burden on your parents of having to support your family,' said Hasnaa. She carried on talking about the heartache and humiliation that she had to face from her friends by marrying someone two years older than her father but kept saying that she had had no choice.

Not only in Syria but in countries like Yemen, Libya, Somalia and Sudan, poverty exacerbated by violence has created a fertile environment for an increase in child and early teenage marriage, with reports of many young girls being forced into marriage because their families desperately needed money. Some accounts suggest that large families may see in their teenage daughters a solution to their own economic problems and a means of escaping refugee camps. Preliminary evidence further indicates that parents may in fact resort to child or early teenage marriage, usually to an older male relative, in order to safeguard a daughter's sexuality or hide the fact that she has been raped (Cetorelli, 2014). Another study done in Lebanon that also interviewed teenage Syrian refugee girls found that the majority of them wanted to continue their education before fleeing Syria, but early marriage emerged as their only way out of impoverishment, dire circumstances, poor housing conditions, with very restricted and irregular income sources (Economic and Social Commission for Western Asia, 2015, p. 57). Conflict and displacement had devastating effects on their educational opportunities.

It was interesting to report a few statements from refugee students saying that they would like to change how some Westerners perceive Arabs and show them that there are good and bad people in all countries, cultures, religions and nationalities. Also, they were asked what makes them think that such perceptions exist and some examples of what has been shared during the interviews demonstrated that many tended to stereotype refugees as terrorists, extremists and lazy. Mohsin gave an example of a situation in Australia while on the train going to school when he heard a conversation between two passengers across from him talking about the girl wearing the hijab and said, 'We should make them take that thing off when they come to live here and make them convert from Islam to keep the peace.' Mohsin was very hurt and wanted to explain to them that it should be up to people to wear what they feel comfortable in, because a hijab does not make someone a bad person at all and being Muslim is not an evil thing. Another similar comment was made by Ayia when she said, 'I wish that we can accept people for who they are without making judgments over color, religion and nationalities … people get hurt and they shouldn't especially when they are not doing anything wrong.' Similarly in Sweden, Hiba mentioned being embarrassed when asked about her religion and felt unsafe to say that she was Muslim. These few examples can be improved throughout education especially if dealt with carefully in schools.

Counsellors and psychologists

Taylor and Sidhu (2012) asserted that it is critical to focus on the importance of realising how different, varied and exceptional the needs of refugee children are. Therefore, speaking with teachers, principals, counsellors and psychologists, their perspectives had to be respected and especially their suggestions regarding what strategies need to be implemented to cater for the needs of these refugee students, their equitable access to schooling, support services being made available and targeting those factors that could strengthen their educational, physical, social and emotional well-being.

A social worker in one Swedish school was keen to provide information on what went on there. According to him:

> I have worked at this school for twelve years. I try to help as a median between the teachers and the students. I help with the language barrier at times and solve problems at other times. I have schedule classroom activities; I work with different groups from different cultures. Students need more help than what we are currently offering them. The teachers can't manage everything by themselves. Students face many issues while seeking education here. They have reading, writing problems and psychological issues which requires so much time and support.

In another school the psychologist provided us with some information on the challenges faced and noted,

> Here we have 45–50 languages; I have learned Somali to speak to some and Arabic to speak to others. Before the holidays we had a problem getting a translator and I offered to learn Afghani. It was emphasised to me that integration depends on the student background, some find it hard to fit into our society.

One female counsellor said that many students feel safer knowing that they have someone who can listen to them without judging them. The psychologist agreed with this statement and commented, 'Most students that have been through our school tend to love it. They don't think of us as only teachers, counsellors and psychologists but they tell us that we are family. They visit us after moving to the mainstream school.' In another school the counsellor believed that his job was 'to talk to students and discuss what seems to be bothering them and talk about teaching them how to process things and make meanings out of the new life in order to plan their future'. It was also mentioned that some refugee students do not know if they will remain permanently in Sweden, and this uncertainty created angst and instability.

In Australia, refugee students were experiencing similar challenges, especially those who arrived illegally in the country and were living in camps. Meanwhile, other refugees who followed the country's immigration and asylum-seeking protocols were granted legal visa status and were subsequently allowed to live and stay in Australia. The majority of Syrian refugee students we talked to were here with their families except for a small number who had lost their parents during the civil war. Counsellors in Australian schools were approached and shared some of their views about the sad state into which some refugee children have fallen and the traumas they still remember. These professionals are very aware of the experiences that have occurred during and that have sadly disrupted a child's natural process of cognitive, emotional, social and physical development. Many school counsellors have to work through the long-term impact of civil war and disruption on these developmental processes, increasing a child's vulnerability to ongoing mental, physical and social problems. The trauma reactions counsellors have encountered include anxiety, loss of control, helplessness, shame and/or guilt, loss of relationships with parents, family and their ethnic community and shattered assumptions about human existence. Maladaptive behaviours sometimes displayed by refugee children in Australian schools have been commonly misinterpreted as misbehaviour and even misdiagnosed as 'borderline personality disorder' or 'antisocial personality' (Nickerson et al., 2016). It is important that such behaviours are understood and taken into consideration in any assessment or treatment interventions.

One psychologist working in an independent school said, 'The two brothers here who lost their parents during the war, at my school tell me that they can't feel happiness. They go out in the streets and they always feel empty. They feel sad and lonely.' A counsellor from another school mentioned that he often talks to refugee students who are somehow distracted and cannot focus on their work and tell them that 'they were so lucky to come to Australia in comparison to where some other people end up going'. In another school, a female mentor shared her experiences and stated at length:

> I try to motivate them to stay at school and get an education. I meet a lot of them in our school, the majority are doing well and getting good grades. I

had a student who came to see me, she was told that she needs to do physics, maths, and English for a year and then go to university. She is very bright and in a year's time when her language improves she will fly. Many of them don't have qualifications from Syria and therefore can't go far without starting from scratch. It is awful for them.

It was disturbing to hear from some refugee students that many choose not to speak to anyone at all and try to deal with their challenges on their own because they feel embarrassed or feel scared to open up to others.

Feelings about their host country

Since 2012, when the uprising in Syria was closely followed by unrest in Libya and Egypt, European nations and Australia have welcomed increasing numbers of refugees who have endured many challenges while trying to integrate into the host society. Due to these challenges, refugees are often resettled multiple times. A major consequence of this is how refugees conceive of what is 'home' and the relationship between people and place, which are especially important in the refugee context due to their forced displacement experienced before arriving in the host country. What Brun (2001, p. 15) wrote nearly 20 years ago is still valid today: 'The way space and place are conceptualized, applied and expressed within the field of refugees studies and in policy work are important for how refugees are understood and represented.' Understanding the 'home' concept has been implied in this book rather than directly addressed, and it remains an essential aspect of research on refugees and asylum seekers. What are the factors that can contribute to achieving a 'home' feeling in the host-country environment? One recent analysis on conditions in Norway (Kohut, 2018) contended that when focusing specifically on housing and refugees' personal perceptions on the concept of 'home', refugees responded to resettlement in various ways: most were basically satisfied with their housing while still referring to their past homes with a 'then and now' dichotomy and a longing for family and former neighbours. Safety and security were recurring themes, especially for families, but other equally important matters in order to feel at home and gain a feeling of belonging were social inclusion, acceptance and understanding of local regulations and ways of doing things. An example of such a situation was discussed by Omar who said,

> Sweden is a beautiful place and many people are lovely and kind to us. My host family treats me very well but it doesn't stop me from wanting to be with my parents. My brother is also here in Sweden and seems happy with his host family but lives many kilometres away in the wood somewhere and I miss him ... I want to be with him ... he is the only family I have in Sweden. He cries and tells me that he is isolated and does not even get to hear anyone ever speak Arabic where he is.

Scholars argue that the process of integration is a complex and multidimensional one, and it can mean different things to different people depending on their interests and perceptions (Korac, 2003). Understanding the meaning of what it feels to be integrated or assimilated into another society is complex but nonetheless important for scholars and policy makers: it will help them to set clear goals, plan appropriate strategies and activities as well as evaluate results. The term 'integration' is widely discussed among scholars, policy makers, the public and media, but is in fact a loaded term. What is meant by and understood here varies significantly among people in society and depends on their own interests and perceptions. Schibel et al. (2002, cited in Kohut, 2018, p. 8) point out that integration is 'a word, used by many but understood differently by most'. At the same time, scholars emphasise that the concept of integration is poorly defined; it is also a chaotic, contested and contextual term (Berry, 2012; Korac, 2013). Integration is in reality a complex process, where numerous actors are involved ranging from individuals, refugee communities, the nation-state, different institutions/agencies/departments, etc.

Comprehending the meaning of integration and the difficulty of achieving will help policy makers and policy implementers set clear goals, plan the right strategies and activities as well as evaluate the outcomes. Various academic studies on refugee integration have suggested there are several characteristics that define the integration process and reflect its meaning. Firstly, integration is a 'two-way process', which indicates the willingness of a host society to accept and adapt to changes (Strang and Ager, 2010). However, it should not be confused with the process of assimilation, where refugees assimilate and this is due to the host country's expectation that they fully accept and live by its culture and customs (Bhugra and Becker, 2005). Secondly, the integration process is multidimensional in character due to a variety of issues and interconnected processes related to integration. Thirdly, the point should be made that refugee children's integration into Western schooling, to take one example, is in effect a non-linear process – it does not necessarily proceed evenly from one stage to another in a predicted, logical way, which is how government policy makers and bureaucracies would like their edicts to work. Finally, integration is a rather subjective process, where refugees and what they want should play a major role as they may find a way to realise their ambitions without drawing on the resources of the host country. For example, refugees should have a right to make decisions about how they want to integrate: at what pace and to what extent (Valtonen, 2004).

On this theme of integration and according to this study's interviewees, female students said that they were told to go back home if they were going to wear the hijab. According to one female student who spoke at length on this issue:

> When you speak broken Swedish, the people make fun of you, they don't see that people have different accents. There is a lot of ignorance, the racism became much higher in the last few years. It is a very high percentage and no

one was expecting it. The media plays a big role and a lot of things to do with it to make people hate them. They say that refugees are getting this much money, refugees rape others, refugees get home. The facts are different and this is not true. Maybe yes they get money when they come here but to help them establish. Politics is becoming awful. They don't see that children here who are Swedish get the same help. They connect one to one, hospitals are closing in north so if people need help they need to travel for miles and they are blaming this on refugees because they are saying that the money is going to them. The media plays a very dirty role.

This theme was picked up on by one teacher who stated,

We have a problem here in the school with students who are all newcomers or refugees who pick on each other. They pick on one another by looking at their colors. So he is black and I am white that means I am better than him and so it goes. We try to educate them and tell them that colors do not make any difference or give one person more rights than another.

The children who we spoke to made it clear that they did not have a say in choosing where they could go to live in Sweden. As mentioned previously, many children were upset because they were separated from their siblings, close family members and friends; Maya said, 'I only wanted to be close to my cousin, he can keep me company and protect me. We are at least four hours away from each other which makes it impossible to see him more than once a month.' Equally, Ihab shook his head with disappointment and stuttered a few words first and then stated more loudly,

The biggest issue for me is that my brothers have been sent away from me, they live three hours away and we can't drive to go see each other because of our age. I have to sit on the train for three hours to get to Oumar and another 2 hours to get to Wael which makes it impossible to see both in one day especially that we have to be back with our host family before ten in the evening every night ... it is impossible and so unfair.

A psychologist also highlighted the fact that when the children arrive they do not have a say in where they are sent to. The decisions were made by the migration centres that hand them over to the community that will allocate them a home. The psychologist said

maybe they get Stockholm, Buden and then the commune puts them in homes so the social services are who does it. We also have camps for different security scales. So if you have a lot of trouble you will live with an educated personnel to provide the student with the support needed.

He carried on saying,

> When we had a lot of people coming, refugees and a lot of youth they had places to live for them. They had families for children and camps that were not good for them; while now the situation is more stable, they make changes and improvement. I think most of them are very happy here.

Refugee children's thoughts about the future

Asking the refugee students the important question of where they see themselves in five years' time was a little confronting for many of our interviewees. The way their eyes twitched made it obvious that their minds were working at full speed in trying to answer this one. A large number of refugee students in Australia who we interviewed remained steadfast that they would stay in this country, attend school until Year 12 and then go to a vocational college or university to learn a trade or other profession in order to obtain good qualifications. This is a long-term strategy and they would have to get less qualified work if they want to earn money more quickly. A few Syrian refugee girls in Australia were not sure of what to say and a small percentage said that they might be married in a few years' time. The legal age for marriage in Australia is 16 for females with parental consent and 18 for females without parental consent. However, since 2017, as stated by the Attorney-General's Department (2018), the minimum legal marriage is 18 but emancipated minors between the age of 16 and 18 have an exception to marry legally. Most refugee children were very happy living in Australia and spoke openly about their feelings without hesitation or any worries. Shadia said, 'I am very lucky to be here, if I was somewhere else I would have to get married at the age of 14 or 15 like most girls from my village. While here in Australia, I am protected by the law and can continue my studies and have a career.' Also Nagee, when asked the question of where he saw himself in five years, sighed and replied, 'I am so happy in Australia and will never leave, especially, that it is so safe here and my parents are happy and settled. We don't have to run around any more and we are no longer scared and finally we have started living like normal people.' This was extremely touching, as we generally do not take the time to understand how much it takes out of people to be displaced, unsafe and unsure.

In Sweden, however, the majority of refugee students who we interviewed asserted that they may migrate somewhere else one day, so it is evident here that the country would not be their final host abode. A few others shared their wish to go to the United States because some have family members already residing there and our interviewees assumed that, being such a wealthy and generally 'open' country, they could have better opportunities to find meaningful jobs and financial security. Only a few students said they would like to go back to Syria to be with their parents, for example Maya, who remarked that she felt lost away from her mother and siblings. Kareem, who is 17 years of age, was disappointed with the lack of freedom in Sweden generally, and said that they needed to be home by ten o'clock every night or they would be in trouble with the police because there is a curfew in place. According to Kareem, living with guardians was too controlling and he needed to live his life like an adult and not as if he was a child. He added that living in Sweden is probably the hardest way of life to come to grips with in the entire world. This was a very interesting point considering its supposed freedoms; according to him, it was difficult because you always need to answer to every little thing that you do to new people that have taken your family's place in your life. Ahmed, who turned 18 at the time of the interview, disagreed with this assertion and said that he has his freedom but one day he may leave and go to the United Kingdom to live with his aunt and uncle and be amongst family and friends. A few girls smiled and said they were relieved because they did not have to be traditional and get married instead of choosing to work.

All refugee children living in Lebanon who we interviewed generally had the same point of view that they would leave Lebanon to go to Europe or other Western countries and were praying to get selected, but the civil war in Syria may lead to a situation where they can never return due to circumstances or government policy. A few Syrian refugee children interviewed in Lebanon mentioned that they are not very comfortable. They sensed that their teachers do not like them and neither do the Lebanese students. Meanwhile, a few others said that they were happy and they enjoyed going to school. Their biggest fear was that they may have to go back home to Syria if politics and policies changed.

Students from refugee backgrounds face many challenges as a result of their previous and often traumatic life experiences, which can distinctly affect their successful transition in Australian and Swedish schools. Recognising that there is no overarching schooling strategy that would entirely successfully support these children, the complexities of each individual refugee student's situation must precede any all-encompassing school support programme if positive outcomes are to be achieved. While a number of school-based support systems and other programmes have been established and reported as successful, more research is needed to identify and actually advise on the implementation of best practices so that students from a Syrian refugee background can progress in life.

For both Australia and Sweden, the challenges that emerged in the interviews with students, teachers and counsellors/psychologists can be summarised as follows:

- Language barriers in meeting educational needs (lack of support bilingual staff).
- Educational needs cannot be separated from social and emotional needs.
- Teachers require ongoing support staff in classrooms for learning and language assistance (preferably Arabic-speaking).
- Time constraints impede teachers' ability to teach all students equally to the required level.

- Teachers require ongoing training to understand how to best support refugee children and their families, especially if counselling services are not available.
- Specific funding set aside for teacher and classroom support services.
- It is important to provide home-language lessons in classrooms so that refugee students can be comfortable, more emotionally secure and encouraged to continue keeping their 'mother-country' language alive, since it is a very important part of their identity.
- Parental involvement in the school and the education of their children is sometimes lacking, due to the issues that parents themselves need to deal with.
- More emphasis needs to be put on community building by encouraging refugee children to feel that they belong.
- Education policy generally on the issue of refugee education is reactive, piecemeal and not well integrated given that national governments and regional or state governments have different (and often competing) policies and procedures.

References

Anderson, Sulome (2016). 'Syria's Refugee Children Have Lost All Hope'. *FP*, 1 June. Retrieved 6 February 2019 from https://foreignpolicy.com/2016/06/29/syrias-refugee-children-have-lost-all-hope/.

Attard, Monica (2015). 'Syrian Refugee Crisis: We're Failing to Do Our Part'. *Drum*, 7 September. Retrieved 5 February 2019 from www.abc.net.au/news/2015-09-07/attard-were-not-stepping-up-to-the-plate-on-syria/6755154.

Attorney-General's Department (2018). 'Getting Married'. Retrieved 10 February 2019 from www.ag.gov.au/FamiliesAndMarriage/Marriage/Pages/Getting-married.aspx.

Berry, S.E. (2012). 'Integrating Refugees: The Case for a Minority Rights Based Approach', *International Journal of Refugee Law*, 24(1), 1–36.

Bhugra, Dinesh and Becker, Matthew A. (2005). 'Migration, Cultural Bereavement and Cultural Identity'. *World Psychiatry*, 4(1), 18–24. Retrieved 7 February 2019 from www.ncbi.nlm.nih.gov/pubmed/16633496.

Brun, C. (2001). 'Reterritorializing the Relationship between People and Place in Refugee Studies'. *Geografiska Annaler: Series B, Human Geography*, 83(1), 15–25.

Cetorelli, Valeria (2014). 'The Effect on Fertility of the 2003–2011 War in Iraq'. *Population and Development Review*, 40(4), 581–604.

Crul, Maurice, Keskiner, E., Schneider, J., Lelie, F. and Ghaeminia, S. (2017). 'No Lost Generation? Education for Refugee Children: A Comparison between Sweden, Germany, the Netherlands and Turkey' (pp. 62–79). In Rainer Baubock and Milena Tripkovic (eds), *The Integration of Migrants and Refugees: An EUI Forum on Migration, Citizenship and Demography*. Retrieved 26 January 2019 from: www. knjiznica.sabor.hr/pdf/E_publikacije/.

Economic and Social Commission for Western Asia (2015). *Child Marriage in Humanitarian Settings in the Arab Region Dynamics, Challenges and Policy Options*. New York: United Nations.

eTwinning (2017). 'New Group on the Community: Integrating Migrant Students at School'. 13 October. Retrieved 7 February 2019 from www.etwinning.net/en/pub/highlights/new-group-on-the-community-in.htm.

Fanjul, Gonzalo, Mansour-Ille, D. et al. (2018). *Migration as an Opportunity: Evidence of Labour Migration Initiatives*. Briefing note. London: Overseas Development Institute. Retrieved 7 February 2019 from www.odi.org/sites/odi.org.uk/files/resource-documents/12308.pdf.

Fernando, Chandi and Ferrari, Michel (2011). 'Spirituality and Resilience in Children of War in Sri Lanka'. *Journal of Spirituality in Mental Health*, 13(1), 52–77.

Hall, Andy and Summers, Hannah (2018). 'Syrian Refugee Children Enjoy a New Start at School – in Pictures'. *Guardian*, 18 November. Retrieved 6 February 2019 from www.theguardian.com/global-development/gallery/2018/nov/13/syrian-refugee-children-enjoy-a-new-start-at-school-in-pictures.

Houghton, Anne-Marie (ed.) (2011). 'Creating and Sustaining International Connections: Exploring the Learning Opportunities for Studying Creative Understandings about Teaching and Research for Equity and Access'. Proceedings of the 41st Annual Conference, University of Lancaster, United Kingdom, 5–7 July.

Kohut, Nadiya (2018). *Perception of Home among Refugees and Integration Process*. Master's thesis, Faculty of Landscape and Society. Norway: Department of International Environment and Development Studies. Retrieved 7 February 2019 from https://brage.bibsys.no/xmlui/bitstream/handle/11250/2495669/Kohut_master_2018.pdf?sequence=4&isAllowed=y.

Korac, M. (2003). 'Integration and How We Facilitate It: A Comparative Study of the Settlement Experiences of Refugees in Italy and the Netherlands'. *Sociology*, 37(1), 51–68.

Lindberg Brekke, C. (2015). *Syrian Refugees in Lebanon's Public School System: Structural and Political Limits for Access*. Oslo: University of Oslo. Retrieved 21 February 2019 from www.duo.uio.no/bitstream/handle/10852/45516/Syrian-Refugees-in-Lebanons-Public-Shool-System.pdf?sequence=1.

McIntyre, Joanna (2017). 'Refugees Welcome? How UK and Sweden Compare on Education for Young Migrants'. *Conversation*, 1 June. Retrieved 18 November 2018 from http://theconversation.com/refugees-welcome-how-uk-and-sweden-compare-on-education-for-young-migrants-74939.

MEHE (2016). *Lebanon Crisis Response Plan 2015–2016*. Lebanon: UNICEF.

Nickerson, Angela, Cloitre, Marylene, Bryant, Richard A., Schnyder, Ulrich, Morina and Schick, Matthias (2016). 'The Factor Structure of Complex Posttraumatic Stress Disorder in Traumatized Refugees'. *European Journal of Psychotraumatology*, 7(1). doi: doi:10.3402/ejpt.v7.33253.

Papadopoulos, Renos K. (2001). 'Refugee Families: Issues of Systemic Supervision'. *Journal of Family Therapy*, 23(4), 405–422.

Rosner, R., Powell, S. and Butollo, W. (2003). 'Posttraumatic Stress Disorder Three Years after the Siege of Sarajevo'. *Journal of Clinical Psychology*, 59(1), 41–55.

Save the Children (2018). *Hear It from the Teachers: Getting Refugee Children Back to Learning*. Fairfield, CT: Save the Children. Retrieved 6 February 2019 from www.savethechildren.org/content/dam/usa/reports/ed-cp/hear-it-from-the-teachers-refugee-education-report.pdf.

Save the Children (n.d.). *Hear It from the Teachers: Getting Refugee Children Back to Learning*. Washington, DC: Save the Children.

Schweitzer, R., MelvilleF., Steel, Z. and Lacherez, P. (2006). 'Trauma, Post-Migration Living Difficulties, and Social Support as Predictors of Psychological Adjustment in

Resettled Sudanese Refugees'. *Australian New Zealand Journal of Psychiatry*, 40(2), 179–187.
Schweitzer, R., Greenslade, J. and Kagee, A. (2007). 'Coping and Resilience in Refugees from the Sudan: A Narrative Account'. *Australian New Zealand Journal of Psychiatry*, 41(3), 282–288.
Secombe, M. and Zajda, J. (eds) (1999). *JJ on Education and Culture*. Albert Park: James Nicholas Publishers.
Shuayb, Maha, Makkouk, Nisrine and Tuttunji, Suha (2014). *Widening Access to Quality Education for Syrian Refugees: The Role of Private and NGO Sectors in Lebanon*. Beirut: Centre for Lebanese Studies.
Smolicz, J.J. (1979). *Culture and Education in a Plural Society*. Canberra: Curriculum Development Centre.
Smolicz, J. and Secombe, M. (1981). *The Australian School through Children's Eyes*. Melbourne: Melbourne University Press.
Spinks, Harriet (2013). 'Destination Anywhere? Factors Affecting Asylum Seekers' Choice of Destination Country'. Research Paper no. 1 2012–2013. Parliament of Australia: Social Policy Section. Retrieved 5 February 2019 from www.aph.gov.au/About_Parliament/Parliamentary_Departments/Parliamentary_Library/pubs/rp/rp1213/13rp01.
Strang, Alison and Ager, Alastair (2010). 'Refugee Integration: Emerging Trends and Remaining Agendas'. *Journal of Refugee Studies*, 23(1), 589–607.
Taylor, S. and Sidhu, R. (2012). 'Supporting Refugee Students in Schools: What Constitutes Inclusive Education?' *International Journal of Inclusive Education*, 16(1), 39–56.
Tiong, A. (2006). 'Health Needs of Newly Arrived African Refugees from a Primary Health Care Perspective'. Retrieved 5 February 2019 from https://scholar.google.com.au/scholar?q=Tiong,+A.+(2006).+Health+needs+of+newly+arrived+African+refugees+from+a+primary&hl=en&as_sdt=0&as_vis=1&oi=scholart.
Tucker, Jason (2018). 'Why Here? Factors Influencing Palestinian Refugees from Syria in Choosing Germany or Sweden as Asylum Destinations'. *Comparative Migration Studies*, 6(1), 29. doi: doi:10.1186/s40878–40018–0094–0092.
Tufan, Ali Evren, Alkin, Melis and Bosgelmez, Sukrive (2012). 'Post-Traumatic Stress Disorder among Asylum Seekers and Refugees in Istanbul May Be Predicted by Torture and Loss due to Violence'. *Nordic Journal of Psychiatry*, 67(3), 219–224.
Valtonen, K. (2004). 'From the Margin to the Mainstream: Conceptualizing Refugee Settlement Processes'. *Journal of Refugee Studies*, 17(1), 70–96.
Wagnild, G.M. and Collins, J.A. (2009). 'Assessing Resilience'. *Journal of Psychosocial Nursing and Mental Health Services*, 47(1), 28–33.
Wångdahl, Josefin (2017). *Health Literacy among Newly Arrived Refugees in Sweden and Implications for Health and Healthcare*. Digital Comprehensive Summaries of Uppsala Dissertations from the Faculty of Medicine 1397. Uppsala Universitet. Retrieved 6 February 2019 from https://uu.diva-portal.org/smash/get/diva2:1158668/FULLTEXT01.pdf.
World Bank (2013). *Building Resilience: Integrating Climate and Disaster Risk into Development*. World Bank Group experience. No. 82648 v2. Washington, DC: World Bank. Retrieved 5 February 2019 from http://documents.worldbank.org/curated/en/653931468340471918/pdf/826480WP0v20Bu0130Box379862000UO090.pdf.
Zwi, Karen (2017). 'How We Can Help Refugee Kids to Thrive in Australia'. *Conversation*, 31 May. Retrieved 6 February 2019 from http://theconversation.com/how-we-can-help-refugee-kids-to-thrive-in-australia-75540.

7
CONCLUSION AND RECOMMENDATIONS

Introduction

This chapter summarises the lessons learnt about Syrian refugee children's education in Sweden and Australia, with an overview on how both countries differ but are also similar, and with recommendations made on why and how their refugee education systems could be improved, and what such improvements would produce. The wave of migrants arriving in Europe and Australia fleeing from war or hard living conditions represents both a challenge and a great educational opportunity for the Australian and European school systems. Currently, research and good practice in this field have been mainly developed within the boundaries of national educational politics and policies, addressing distinct populations. While this fragmentation has stood in the way of a systematic analysis of the question at the host-country level, it is a necessary condition for investigating and implementing successful educational interventions as they apply to refugee populations. The provision of education for refugees is a vast and complex topic. Once access to schooling is ensured, as this study has found, equity and quality are vital areas that need to be addressed. While Australia and Sweden have introduced and formulated strategies to ensure that Syrian refugees can attend school, the high numbers still not accessing educational opportunities indicate the need for urgent action. Indeed, the education of refugee children raises many strategic questions: for example, should longer-term measures be implemented to allow refugee children to follow the host country's curriculum? Or, should parallel systems be set up for children to follow an adapted Syrian curriculum? The first takes for granted that they settle permanently in the host country, while the second assumes that they will return eventually to Syria or at least an Arabic-speaking country.

Education is an essential aspect of people's settlement in another country. Increasingly, it is recognised that education and schools support the health and well-being of refugee children in English-speaking countries like Australia and English-language tuition is valuable for new arrivals with low English proficiency (Kirk and Cassity, 2007; Rousseau and Guzder, 2008; Correa-Velez et al., 2010). More broadly, the motivation and potential demonstrated by many children and people of refugee backgrounds offer a convincing argument for developing more flexible and innovative strategies for participation in education. The evidence from Australia and Sweden is that specific support is required to ensure Syrian refugee-background students reach their full educational and social potential. Both countries provide access from primary to tertiary education for refugee entrants and people granted permanent protection. Refugee-background children and adolescents face significant educational but also psychological disadvantage due to their refugee experience, migration and language transitions (Fazel and Stein, 2002).

General findings for Australia and Sweden

The rationale for choosing Australia and Sweden for this study on the schooling experiences of Syrian 'children of war' is based on both nations having become increasingly ethnically and racially very diverse over the last 30 years, due in part to their governments' pursuing much more liberal immigration and refugee policies (Castles, 1995, pp. 293–5). They are in fact examples of countries where large-scale migrations have led to different responses. As stated at the beginning of this book, the 1951 Refugee Convention stipulates that refugees should not be penalised for their illegal entry or stay; however, the protection of asylum seekers does depend on whether or not the host state respects its international obligations under the Convention and international law. Australia was one of the first countries to become a state party to the Refugee Convention in January 1954, and nearly 20 years later to the 1967 Protocol Relating to the Status of Refugees in December 1973. Sweden's accession to both the Convention and Protocol occurred respectively in October 1954 and October 1967. As signatories to the Refugee Convention, both countries are obliged to protect the rights of refugees and uphold their legal responsibilities towards them. However, in recent years, unlike Sweden, Australia has to some extent ignored its obligations to asylum seekers and, instead, constructed the issue of asylum into a national security one for political parties' electoral advantage. In contrast, Sweden received the highest number of asylum seekers per capita in 2014, and maximised its ability to process and host them in 2015; its government has rejected any construction of the refugee/asylum issue in terms of security, threat or criminality (De Silva, 2017, pp. 1–2).

This is only part of the institutional background that the study carried out, highlighting the subtle and not-so-subtle differences between Australia and Sweden in their treatment of Syrian refugee children trying to obtain an education. Another equally important part of the context is that in both countries, schools and teachers are no longer seen as agents of change but as agents of society; this is reflected in successive policy shifts relating to funding and outcomes-based assessment, as well as heightened teacher accountability to the vicissitudes of parents' and communities' expectations. The shift in education policies has been influenced by what Taylor (2008, p. 60) terms 'neoliberal global policy trends, resulting in reduced education funding, reduced commitment to humanitarian aid and resettlement of refugees, and a general marginalisation of concerns about equity and social justice in education'. Nonetheless, it is clearly evident that teachers and schools in both countries want to provide Syrian refugee children with educational contexts that foster their well-being and overcome feelings and realities of vulnerability. What has been referred to by Zembylas (2010) as an 'ethic of care' has emerged in response to the particular circumstances that Syrian refugee children and their families face. Kum describes this quality as focusing on 'trust, social bonds, cooperation, caring relations, and responding to needs' (2017, p. 136), and situates it within the characteristics of inclusive and democratic societal practice. Such an ethic is directly in contrast with the contemporary climate of government policy and corresponding attitudes in the wider community. The interviews that formed a substantial part of this study have suggested that an ethic of care is especially important in the developmentally sensitive first years of a refugee child's education in another country (Reed et al., 2012), yet, we still have much to research on the characteristics of schools that are most supportive of young refugee children and their families (Szente et al., 2006; Waniganayake, 2001).

Sweden emerges as the more responsive country when integrating refugee immigrants, which could actually be hanging in the balance given that the far-right Sweden Democrats party won almost 18 percent of the votes in the 2018 election (Kantor, 2018). It appears that Syrian families like those of Alana Abdallah, who lives in the neighbourhood of Gullvik in the coastal city of Malmö, have been subjected to increasing xenophobic crimes, with a once progressive immigration policy now tightened up with a retroactive law to send people back to their home country if it was considered safe to do so. From 2012 to 2016, xenophobic hate crimes in Sweden increased by 16 percent, and Islamophobic crimes by 43 percent for the same period. In 2016 alone, more than 90 arson attacks on asylum centres were reported (Kantor, 2018). This is an issue that already complicates the educational opportunities for refugee and asylum-seeking children, which can be summarised as follows:

- lack of clarity in the Compulsory School Ordinance as to who should receive Swedish as a second language and study guidance in the mother tongue;
- lack of resources in the number of schools able to provide suitable and adequate tuition and guidance for refugee and asylum-seeking children;
- difficulties in dealing with students from diverse backgrounds and existence of perhaps too much variation in levels of prior schooling;

110 Conclusion and recommendations

- great challenges in dealing with traumatised children; and
- low status of Swedish as second language teachers coupled by the need for them to have appropriate teacher training with respect to working in a multicultural setting.

Newcomers have the same rights and measures that guarantee access to pre-primary, compulsory and vocational education, which targets their particular education needs, provides lessons in their mother tongue and the necessary support for making intercultural education possible. Furthermore, Sweden's municipalities and schools are responsible for ensuring that newcomers obtain Sweden as a second language and are expected to take initiatives to provide individualised support addressing specific needs so that progress to an equivalent academic level as the Swedes is made (MIPEX, 2015; Rothschild, 2016). Swedish Tuition for Immigrants is the most widely utilised programme that permits refugees and other immigrants to take language courses for free, in order to integrate more effectively into society. Refugees also receive unwavering educational support from the National Education Board (Skolverket) in gaining access to education and language-learning opportunities (Egerstrom, 2016). The degree of support displayed by the Swedish government is visible in its efforts to incorporate retired teachers into school systems, to help cope with the large volumes of pupils and engage in training programmes for English-speaking refugees. Such initiatives boost refugee integration, as they are now educated in their mother tongues (Egerstrom, 2016). Although the Swedish introduction to education is supportive, some obstacles such as feelings of segregation and dissatisfying preparatory classes, due to inadequacy of teaching in their respective mother tongues, hinder effective integration of newcomers.

In addition, complex psychological needs of unaccompanied minors and poor communication between the school systems and the Migration Agency have created issues for local authorities to organise and effectively include refugee children into the country's education system. The arrival of refugees has caused a strain on the Swedish government, with a shortage in staff for educating newcomers (Fratzke, 2016). Swedish research has found it is difficult to predict or gather insights into the possible outcomes of the policy practices implemented by the Swedish authorities (Bunar, 2010). However, Crul (n.d., pp. 3–5) outlined the following recommendations based on research done in Sweden, Germany, the Netherlands and Turkey, and they are viable for Sweden: firstly, access to and beyond compulsory school; secondly, institute a policy of immersion classes and the tracking of refugee students' progress in learning the Swedish language; thirdly, performance and tracking in terms of vocational aptitudes and cognitive skills; and fourthly, upward and downward streaming after the age of 15, whereby refugee students can still grow and upgrade their learning skills despite initial failure.

The Swedish National Agency for Education must improve its communication to schools and municipalities, in order to aid the adjustment of refugees into schools and other educational institutions. It is important to note that many of the children enrolled are unaccompanied minors and, therefore, these children encounter more difficulty in integrating into the education system. At times many of them have been travelling for two or three years and therefore have been unable to attend school, or have not been in any form of educational background and require special attention and measures towards grasping a new language, adapting to the school curriculum and, most importantly, adapting to the educational environment once again. Moreover, some students may lag behind natives because they do not have the necessary educational knowledge to match pupils of a similar age, and therefore have to join younger years (Crul, 2017).

In Australia, access and participation for refugee students in the public education system have been compromised by poor transition strategies, with teachers feeling ill-equipped and under-resourced to provide the requisite educational and psychosocial support for the growing numbers of refugee arrivals (Cassity and Gow, 2005; Miller et al., 2005). In many cases, too, teachers do not have formal and/or adequate training in ESL, in curriculum making for refugee students and/or in relevant cultural sensitivity studies. Matthews has claimed that 'Australian schools are poorly funded and ill-equipped to provide effective English as a Second Language teaching and support' (2008, p. 31; see also Taylor, 2008; Sidhu and Taylor, 2007). Moreover, there is a disjunction between initial integration programmes upon arrival – provided by intensive English-language centres for 6–12 months – and support provided after students enter mainstream high school (Christie and Sidhu, 2006, p. 457; Olliff and Couch, 2005).

In contrast, government support for refugee education is often lacking. In New South Wales, for example, which receives about 40 percent of the nation's refugee intake, restricted resource allocations seriously undermine the amount of language and literacy support available (Refugee Council of Australia, 2010, p. 40; Iredal and Fox, 1997, p. 655). There is a real need for increased mediation and reporting on students to ensure that long-term welfare, language, and health needs are addressed across Australia (Cassity and Gow, 2005, p. 55). Research shows that refugee students can often be lost within the broader Australian school community and accordingly may not have their special needs met in an education system driven by market forces and school-based resource allocation. Sidhu and Taylor have scrutinised Australian 'New Arrival' programmes and found that, nationally, refugee needs are commonly conflated with those of other ESL students (2007, p. 288). Creagh (2014), too, shows how in the disaggregation of school test data refugees can be included in a Language Background Other than English category. As this grouping also includes students who may be proficient in English but have non-English-speaking parents, the refugee can be 'rendered invisible' in testing, policy and curriculum making (Creagh et al., 2013). Refugees face distinct and specific issues that impact on educational attainments, including interrupted learning, experience of trauma and concerns about legal status and family welfare (Stevenson and Willott, 2007, p. 671; Woods, 2009,

p. 81). Moreover, these individuals arrive with little conception of the history, culture, principles and practices of the host country.

In an era of contracting resource allocation, schools must ensure that curriculum design and development follows best practice to ensure that the unique learning needs of refugees receive appropriate support. The Refugee Council of Australia (2018) has highlighted the many challenges faced by young refugees in 'making the transition to life in Australia, particularly with regards to their pursuit of education and training' (p. 3) Strategies for overcoming these challenges in practical educational and social settings – such as through targeted curriculum making for high schools – have not been addressed. Taylor summarises the potential pathways for refugee support when, in her examination of education policy for refugees in Queensland and Australia more generally, she concludes: 'schools could play a crucial role in supporting transitions to belonging and citizenship for refugee young people, but … this will require more support from governments and systems in the form of appropriate policies and strategies, and the provision of adequate resources' (Taylor, 2008, p. 58).

Sweden and Australia are examples of countries where alternatives to detention are now considered a significant global countertrend to the normalisation of detaining migrants. Where such alternatives had been put into action, they have relied on migrants themselves to be active participants in the immigration process. It has been noted that both Sweden and Australia have successfully developed alternatives to detention based on case management in the community (International Detention Coalition, 2009; Phelps, 2013, pp. 45–6), which includes early intervention and individual assessment, and the key feature is preparing, supporting and empowering individuals. In both countries, independent legal advice, welfare assistance and community organisations' active involvement are key elements of the immigration pathway. It is evident that case managers spend time with migrants building relationships of trust, exploring long-term options and possibilities in third countries (Ernst and Young, 2015).

This leads to another area where Swedish and Australian policies are similar – the context of language-learning participation rates and mentorship. Both countries not only invest considerable resources in language classes, but also know what proportion of their immigrant populations participate in these programmes. Only Australia, the Canadian province of British Columbia, Finland, the Netherlands and Sweden are able to provide figures for participation rates. In Australia and Sweden, about 33 percent of newly arrived immigrants attend the voluntary language-learning programmes. It is important to note here, however, that the Australia estimate covers all newcomers to the country, not only those eligible for or requiring English-language tuition. To meet the visa requirements if they are entering under the skilled worker category, immigrants to Australia must come from English-speaking countries or be able to demonstrate a functional level of English-language proficiency (OECD, 2006, pp. 125–6). With reference to mentoring, Australia and Sweden encourage a mentorship system to help refugees identify job opportunities, draft CVs, prepare for interviews, etc. The general experience is, however, as shown in the previous chapters, that such programmes have to be set up and run locally when support from the national government in terms of funding or resourcing is not forthcoming (Keeley, 2009, pp. 104–5).

Recommendations

Based on the results and interpretation of various forms of data acquired for this research, the following recommendations are made for policy makers in both Sweden and Australia when introducing Syrian refugee children to their education systems:

- Remove all the legal barriers that prevent or impede access to education, irrespective of their migration status and especially if they are unaccompanied asylum seekers ranging in age from childhood to 18 and older.
- Provide appropriate diagnostic and psychological tests, based on scientifically produced and tested material, on students' previous education background, knowledge and experiences, as well as the adoption of an individual development strategy for each student. It is important that such tests are individualised, with the results properly communicated to all concerned teachers and relevant school/departmental staff.
- Provide bilingual support (Swedish, English and the student's mother tongue) of learning as this kind of support represents a very strong pedagogical instrument that encourages Syrian refugee children to keep learning.
- Ensure there are more teachers with the appropriate training and qualifications who can teach English as a second language in Australia.
- Avoid educational segregation, for instance, no separated classes for an extended period of time, nor schools only for newcomers.
- There has to be a well-planned transfer from introductory to regular classes, and continuous bilingual and social scaffolding in regular classrooms, to promote learning at its best.
- Evaluate refugee children's learning and social-inclusion progress, making sure that this process is continuous and ongoing.
- Make available awareness education for non-immigrant parents to negate the problems raised by stigmatisation and fears of integration, as these can influence Syrian refugee children negatively.
- Provide information and offer good and consistent cooperation to newly arrived Syrian parents on all aspects of schooling.
- Ensure that inquiries into the probable and possible traumatic experiences of Syrian children are professionally and sensitively administered.
- Ensure that schools which have enrolled Syrian children provide opportunities for them to work together with their local community and the wider civic society in order to integrate both adults and children in local social networks.

Final remarks

Documenting the experiences of individuals must take account of the systems and communities that surround refugee resettlement, and of how the social and cultural environment affects each individual's experience of resettlement. Although the themes, processes and outcomes highlighted in the previous chapters will be relevant when examining community factors, researchers and service providers must also understand the macro-level factors independently in order to have a clearer picture of the dynamic and multi-level nature of refugee resettlement and, subsequently, children's education. A critical influence on resettlement is the host country's attitudes towards refugees and their families. Similar to changes that occur within the immigrant individual or group, members of the host society can also vary in the extent to which they maintain their original cultural and ethnic identity and the relationships they seek across groups.

Looking at just Australia, people's attitudes toward newcomers have vacillated over the last 100 years, as evidenced by public policy and community opinions (Neumann, 2004). The discourse surrounding the recently arrived Syrian-conflict refugees has been a divisive one, where at times it has revolved around choosing those from particular religious groups; others have placed an emphasis on the positive net contribution in terms of financial and human capital that families and individuals will make. It is important to state here that evidence throughout Australia's history reveals that both migrants and refugees have made a positive net contribution to Australian society and its economy (Groutsis et al., 2016). Yet it is still the case that the dominant message from the government's perspective is one of engaging in a process of careful refugee selection and administration as a way of creating equal access, 'avoiding queue jumpers' and protecting Australia's borders.

Refugee experiences in Australia and in other countries around the world are arguably linked to the receptions they receive in the host countries. Psychologists need to understand that education interventions for refugee children can only work within systems that recognise and curtail or eliminate experiences of oppression which limit growth and well-being. These influences range from overt prejudice and discrimination to subtle systemic prejudice and discrimination. For instance, employing terminology with specific reference to various ethnic or racial groups can play a role in influencing public attitudes (especially making them judgemental) toward refugees. One such analysis examined the terminology used by media, pointing out that the social categorisation of individuals as 'boat people' and 'illegal immigrants' can encourage marginalising practices (O'Doherty and Le Couteur, 2007).

Education for newly arrived students in Sweden and Australia has developed significantly, if not consistently, during the last years in terms of its quality, organisation, resources, content and supporting structures. What is required in both countries is a sense of clarity in what various levels of government want to achieve, and this means depoliticising the arrival of Syrian refugee children and their families, so that they can fit in with the rest of Swedish and Australian societies. The main stakeholders in the school systems have a much more profound and clear system to work with and follow. There should be clarity on who is accountable for students' achievements, results, ability to integrate into society and be productive citizens, and welfare.

Today, all schools, teachers and principals should become aware that the newly arrived children must be considered and treated as individuals with specific challenges and strengths, that they cannot be automatically placed in various organisational or administrative contexts without closer scrutiny of their background; and that support in their mother tongue and continuing development of their mother tongue is also a prerequisite for learning English and Swedish. The remaining problems to be addressed are, as mentioned above, the social exclusion of the newly arrived from the schools' daily life, the concentration of most newly arrived in only certain schools, the poor relationships between teachers and parents and others in the wider community, the need for employing and assisting language-support teachers, the professional development of all teachers in the area of language development, and in teaching and working in increasingly diverse schools, given that the character of Swedish and Australian schools is much more multicultural and ethnically diverse.

There is, finally, one necessary precondition to fulfil so that newly arrived Syrian refugee children have access to equal opportunities in education and fair opportunities from the beginning. They must be considered and treated in the same way as children born in Australia or Sweden, students in their schools with particular learning needs, and thus the responsibility of all; not as 'temporary others', as refugees and asylum seekers who perhaps will soon be forced to leave the country. Resilience and empowerment of refugee children are crafted from encouraging positive traits in them and reassuring the existence of positive relationships between the newly arrived and the receiving society.

References

Bunar, N. (2010). *Nyanlända och lärande: en forskningsöversikt om nyanlända elever i den svenska skolan* (New Arrivals and Learning: A Research Overview of Newly Arrived Pupils in the Swedish School). Stockholm: Vetenskapsrådet.

Cassity, E. and Gow, G. (2005). 'Shifting Space and Cultural Place: The Transition Experiences of African Young People in West Sydney Schools'. Paper presented at the Australian Association of Educational Research, Annual Conference, Sydney.

Castles, Stephen (1995). 'How Nation-States Respond to Immigration and Ethnic Diversity'. *Journal of Ethnic and Migration Studies*, 21(3), pp. 293–308.

Christie, P. and Sidhu, R. (2006). 'Governmentality and "Fearless Speech": Framing the Education of Asylum Seeker and Refugee Children in Australia'. *Oxford Review of Education*, 32(4), 449–465.

Correa-Velez, I., Gifford, S.M. and Barnett, A.G. (2010). 'Longing to Belong: Social Inclusion and Wellbeing among Youth with Refugee Backgrounds in the First Three Years in Melbourne, Australia'. *Social Science and Medicine*, 71(8), 1399–1408.

Creagh, S. (2014). 'A Critical Analysis of Problems with the LBOTE Category on the NAPLaN Test'. *Australian Educational Researcher*, 41, 1–23.

Creagh, T.A., Nelson, K.J. and Clarke, J.A. (2013). 'A Social Justice Framework for Safeguarding Student Learning Engagement'. In 16th International First Year in Higher Education Conference, 7–10 July, Museum of New Zealand Te Papa Tongarewa, Wellington. Retrieved 26 February 2019 from https://eprints.qut.edu.au/60838/.

Crul, Maurice (2017). *Refugee Children in Education in Europe: How to Prevent a Lost Generation?* SIRIUS Network Policy Brief Series, Issue No. 7. Retrieved 26 October 2018 from www.sirius-migrationeducation.org/wp-content/uploads/2012/06/Refugee-children-in-education-in-Europe.-How-to-prevent-a-lost-generation.pdf.

Crul, Maurice (n.d.). 'Children of Immigrants and Refugees in Europe: Combining Outcomes of PISA Results and Results of Other International Surveys'. Retrieved 26 February 2019 from www.oecd.org/education/school/Maurice-Crul-RD11.pdf.

De Silva, Mary Lynn (2017). *Norm Circles, Stigma and the Securitization of Asylum: A Comparative Study of Australia and Sweden*. Doctoral thesis, University of Western Australia, School of Social Sciences. Retrieved 5 January 2019 from https://api.research-repository.uwa.edu.au/portalfiles/portal/21986470/THESIS_DOCTOR_OF_PHILOSOPHY_DE_SILVA_Mary_Lynn_2017.pdf.

Egerstrom, C. (2016). 'Education: The Key to Integrating Refugees in Sweden', 20 August. Retrieved from www.borgenmagazine.com/education-of-refugees-in-sweden/

Ernst and Young (2015). 'Evaluation of the Humanitarian Settlement Services and Complex Case Support Programmes'. Prepared for the Australian Government Department of Social Services.

Fazel, M. and Stein, A. (2002). 'The Mental Health of Refugee Children'. *Archives of Disease in Childhood*, 87(5), 366–370.

Fratzke, S. (2016). *Forced Migration in the OIC Member Countries: Policy Framework Adopted by Host Countries*. Ankara: COMCEC. Retrieved 16 August 2018 from http://ebook.comcec.org/Kutuphane/Icerik/Yayinlar/Analitik_Calismalar/Yoksullugun_Azaltilmasi/Toplanti8/files/assets/basic-html/page-3.html.

Groutsis, D., O'Leary, J. and Russell, G. (2016). 'Capitalizing on the Cultural and Linguistic Diversity of Mobile Talent: Lessons from an Australian Study'. *International Journal of Human Resource Management*, 29(1), 2231–2252.

International Detention Coalition (2009). 'Case Management as an Alternative to Immigration Detention: The Australian Experience'. June. Retrieved 28 February 2019 from https://idcoalition.org/wp-content/uploads/2009/06/casemanagementinaustralia.pdf.

Iredale, Robyn and Fox, Christine (1997). 'The Impact of Immigration on School Education in New South Wales, Australia'. *International Migration Review*, 31(3), 655–669.

Kantor, Alice (2018). 'Sweden's Shift Right Has Immigrants Worried'. *PRI: Public Radio International*, 29 October. Retrieved 26 February 2019 from www.pri.org/stories/2018-10-29/swedens-shift-right-has-immigrants-worried.

Keeley, Brian (2009). 'Migrants and Work'. In Brian Keeley (ed.),, *International Migration: The Human Face of Globalisation*. Paris: OECD Publishing. Retrieved 28 February 2019 from www.oecd-ilibrary.org/docserver/9789264055780-7-en.pdf?expires=1551316097&id=id&accname=guest&checksum=AED59A69E6821AC84F6DEC5323AA8747.

Kirk, J. and Cassity, E. (2007). 'Minimum Standards for Quality Education for Refugee Youth'. *Youth Studies Australia*, 26(1), 50–56.

Kum, Henry Asei (2017). 'Rhetoric, Reality and Refugees on the Margins: Remoralising the Ethic of Care and the European Union (EU) refugee policies'. *Journal of Education and Social Policy*, 7(1), 129–142.

Matthews, J.M. (2008). 'Schooling and Settlement: Refugee Education in Australia'. *International Studies in Sociology of Education*, 18(1), 31–45.

Miller, J., Mitchell, J. and Brown, J. (2005). 'African Refugees with Interrupted Schooling in the High School Mainstream: Dilemmas for Teachers'. *Prospect*, 20(2), 19–33.

MIPEX (2015). 'Migrant Integration Policy Index'. Barcelona/ Brussels: CIDOB and MPG. Retrieved from www.mipex.eu/.

Neumann, K. (2004). *Refuge Australia: Australia's Humanitarian Record*. Sydney: University of New South Wales Press.

O'Doherty, K. and Le Couteur, A. (2007). '"Asylum Seekers", "Boat People" and "Illegal Immigrants": Social Categorisation in the Media'. *Australian Journal of Psychology*, 59(1), 1–12.

OECD (2006). 'Policies and Practices to Help Immigrant Students Attain Proficiency in the Language of Instruction'. In *Immigrant Students Succeed: A Comparative Review of Performance and Engagement in PISA 2003*. Paris: OECD Publishing. Retrieved 28 February 2019 from www.oecd-ilibrary.org/docserver/9789264023611-7-en.pdf?expires=1551315768&id=id&accname=guest&checksum=03EAB5D4C38808D7419DA74C93F5CA33.

Olliff, L. and Couch, J. (2005). 'Pathways and Pitfalls: The Journey of Refugee Young People in and around the Education System in Greater Dandenong, Victoria'. *Youth Studies Australia*, 24(3), 42–46.

Phelps, Jerome (2013). 'Alternatives to Detention in the UK: From Enforcement to Engagement?' *Forced Migration Review*, 44, 45–48.

Reed, R.V., Fazel, M., Jones, L., Panter-Brick, C. and Stein, A. (2012). 'Mental Health of Displaced and Refugee Children Resettled in Low-Income and Middle-Income Countries: Risk and Protective Factors'. *Lancet*, 379(9812), 250–265.

Refugee Council of Australia (2010) 'Finding the Right Time and Place: Exploring Post-Compulsory Education and Training Pathways for Young People from Refugee Backgrounds in NSW'. Retrieved 16 August 2018 from www.refugeecouncil.org.au/r/rpt/2010-Education.pdf.

Refugee Council of Australia (2018). 'Refugee Alternatives Conference Report'. 9 October. Retrieved 29 February 2019 from www.refugeecouncil.org.au/settling-in-australia/.

Rothschild, Nathalie (2016). 'On the Frontline of Integration: How Swedish Schools Are Helping Refugees'. *Guardian*, 26 June. Retrieved 5 January 2019 from www.theguardian.com/teachernetwork/2016/jun/26/on-the-frontline-of-integration-how-swedish-schools-are-helpingrefugees.

Rousseau, C. and Guzder, J. (2008). 'School-Based Prevention Programs for Refugee Children'. *Child and Adolescent Psychiatric Clinics of North America*, 17(3), 533–549.

Sidhu, R. and Taylor, S. (2007). 'Educational Provision for Refugee Youth in Australia: Left to Chance?' *Journal of Sociology*, 43(3), 283–300.

Stevenson, J. and Willott, J. (2007). 'The Aspiration and Access to Higher Education of Teenage Refugees in the UK'. *Compare: A Journal of Comparative and International Education*, 37(5), 671–687.

Szente, J., Hoot, J. and Taylor, D. (2006). 'Responding to the Special Needs of Refugee Children: Practical Ideas for Teachers'. *Early Childhood Education Journal*, 34(1), 15–20.

Taylor, Sandra C. (2008). 'Schooling and the Settlement of Refugee Young People in Queensland: "… the Challenges Are Massive"'. *Social Alternatives*, 27(3), 58–65.

Waniganayake, M. (2001). 'From Playing with Guns to Playing with Rice: The Challenges of Working with Refugee Children – an Australian Perspective'. *Childhood Education*, 77(5), 289–294.

Woods, A. (2009). 'Learning to Be Literate: Issues of Pedagogy for Recently Arrived Refugee Youth in Australia'. *Critical Inquiry in Language Studies*, 6(1/2), 81–101.

Zembylas, Michalinos (2010). 'The Emotional Aspects of Leadership for Social Justice: Implications for Leadership Preparation Programs'. *Journal of Educational Administration*, 48(5), 611–625.

APPENDIX

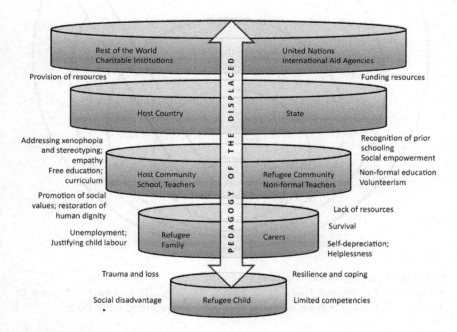

FIGURE A1 Pedagogy of the displaced
Source: Maadad, N. and Rodwell, G. (2017). *Schooling and Education in Lebanon for Syrian and Palestinian Refugees inside and outside the Camps.* Bern: Peter Lang

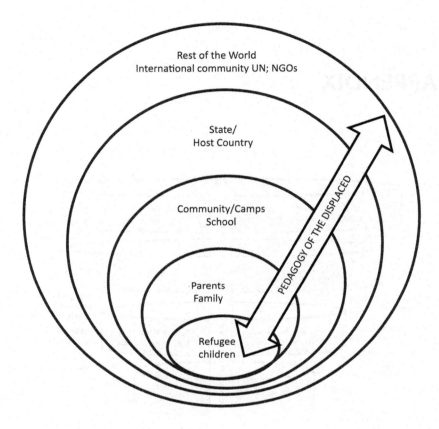

FIGURE A2 Pedagogy of the displaced
Source: Maadad, N. and Rodwell, G. (2017). *Schooling and Education in Lebanon for Syrian and Palestinian Refugees inside and outside the Camps*. Bern: Peter Lang

INDEX

Assimilation 14, 27, 28, 29, 32, 86, 100
Australia refugee programme 47, 48, 50
Australia refugee problem 49
Australian curriculum 55, 63

Boal, A. 15
Bornstein, D. 25
Bangladesh 17

Catholic 31, 60
Children intake 63
Community settlement services 51
Community based initiative 62
Critical paradigm concepts 39, 43

Diversity 29, 55

EALD 54, 55, 56
Education and schooling 19
Education policies 10, 15, 26, 46, 54, 55, 61, 78, 109
Education departments 54
English as a second language 49, 57, 58, 62
European Union 2, 7

Freire, P. 15

Global 3, 9, 10, 32, 38, 52, 54, 61, 77, 109, 112
Globalisation 56, 57

Humanitarian program 51, 52, 53
Humanitarian settlement programs 53, 60, 61

Islamaphobia 30, 31
Intake of refugee 61

Language acquisition 22, 62
Language learning 29, 30, 81, 85, 87, 89, 92, 110, 112
Language support 57, 59, 115
Lebanon 16
Literacy and language 23, 29,

Moral panic 30
Myanmar 17

Opportunities 3, 10, 16, 24, 26, 28, 32, 42, 45, 50, 61, 70, 81, 86, 89, 92, 95, 102, 107, 109–113, 115

Pedagogy of the Oppressed 15, 20, 27, 37, 43
Pedagogy of the Displaced 119
Policies in Australia 72, 78
Policies in Sweden 28, 2
Post-traumatic 79, 80, 94
Political 8, 11, 14, 15, 30, 32, 46, 52, 63, 108
Psychological distress 22
Public education 58, 59, 111
Public schools 16, 50, 55

Rapid Response Education Program 22
Refugee convention 2, 6, 7, 52, 53, 61, 108, 109
Resettlement 4, 8, 22, 49, 51, 52, 73, 74, 81, 98, 109, 114

School policies 10, 15, 26, 46, 54, 55, 61, 78, 109
Settlement 23, 26, 27, 29, 48, 49, 50, 53, 56, 58, 59, 61,
Support services 48, 52, 55, 57, 61, 98, 104
Syrian refugee crisis 3, 4

Theatre of the Oppressed 15, 21, 22, 24, 27, 57

Transformative 21, 25
Trauma 7, 14, 15, 17, 19, 20–24, 26, 28–31, 51, 62, 64
Traumatic 7, 25, 41, 46, 74, 77, 79
Traumatised 15, 17, 18, 22, 24, 25

UNHCR 6, 7, 9, 51, 53
UNICEF 4, 5, 18
United Nations 9, 16, 27,

Violence 4, 17, 22, 26, 45, 90, 96

Welfare system 71, 72
White Australia 47, 48
World war 23, 28, 47, 48, 52